on the wall *contemporary wallpaper*

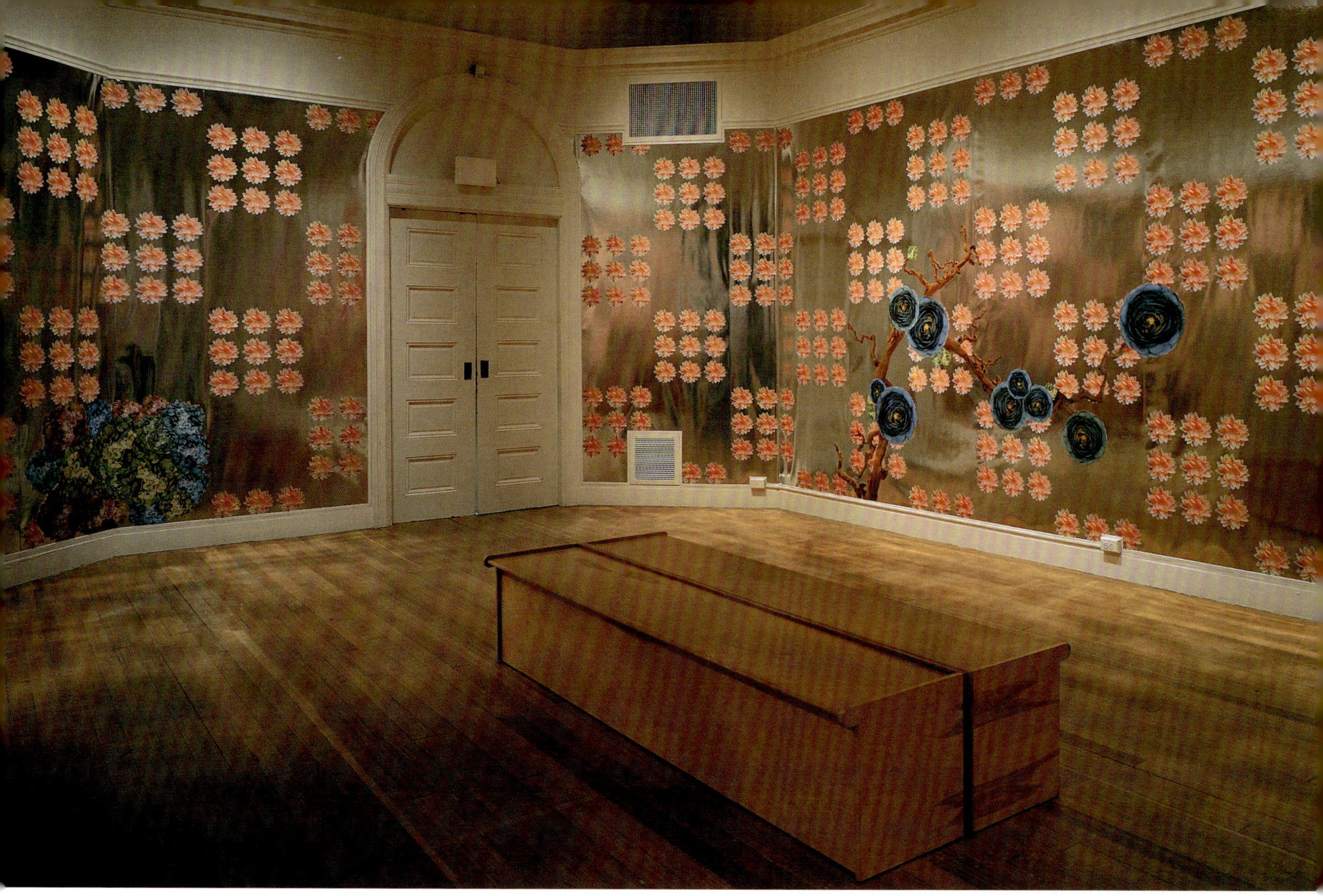

COVER: John Baldessari, *I Will Not Make Any More Boring Art* (wallpaper), 1971/2000, screenprint on paper. Courtesy of the artist and Printed Matter, New York

INSIDE FRONT COVER: Francesco Simeti, *Arabian Nights* (wallpaper), 2003, digital print on paper. Created in collaboration with The RISD Museum. Courtesy of the artist and Galleria Massimo Minini, Brescia

ABOVE: Virgil Marti at RISD, *Lotus Room*, 2003, wallpaper: hand screen-print on Mylar, digital decals. Created in collaboration with the RISD Printmaking Department, The RISD Museum, and The Fabric Workshop and Museum. Courtesy of the artist

Museum of Art
Rhode Island School of Design
224 Benefit Street
Providence, Rhode Island
02903-2723

401-454-6500
www.risdmuseum.org

The Fabric Workshop and Museum
1315 Cherry Street, 5th and 6th Floors
Philadelphia, Pennsylvania
19107-2026

215-568-1111
www.fabricworkshopandmuseum.org

This publication was supported through the generous assistance of The Elizabeth Firestone Graham Foundation.

The exhibition at the Museum of Art, Rhode Island School of Design, was supported by the Bafflin Foundation and Adler's; media sponsor NBC 10.

The exhibition and new works created at The Fabric Workshop and Museum were supported by The Pew Charitable Trusts, Pennsylvania Council on the Arts, National Endowment for the Arts, LLWW Foundation, The Philadelphia Cultural Fund, Independence Foundation, The Claneil Foundation, Miller-Plummer Foundation, The Barra Foundation, and the Board of Directors and members of The Fabric Workshop and Museum.

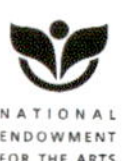

Edited by Judith A. Singsen, The RISD Museum
Designed by Matthew Monk (RISD MFA '91),
for RISD's Design Marketing Collaborative
Printed by Meridian Printing, East Greenwich, Rhode Island

ISBN: 0-911517-75-8

Library of Congress Control Number: 2003106729

JUDITH TANNENBAUM
MARION BOULTON STROUD

on the wall *contemporary wallpaper*

Museum of Art, Rhode Island School of Design, Providence
The Fabric Workshop and Museum, Philadelphia

This catalogue accompanies two exhibitions:

on the wall

wallpaper by contemporary artists

Museum of Art,
Rhode Island School of Design
February 7 – April 20, 2003

Ann Agee
John Baldessari
Matthew Benedict
Brian Chippendale
Adam Cvijanovic
General Idea
Robert Gober
Rodney Graham
Renée Green
Jenny Holzer
Jim Isermann
Virgil Marti
Jane Masters
Takashi Murakami
Joan Nelson
Paul Noble
Jorge Pardo
Francesco Simeti
Do-Ho Suh
Christine Tarkowski
Andy Warhol
Carrie Mae Weems
William Wegman

on the wall

wallpaper and tableau

The Fabric Workshop and Museum
May 9 – September 13, 2003

John Baldessari
Mike Bidlo
Adam Cvijanovic
Drew Dominick
Nicole Eisenman
Viola Frey
General Idea
Robert Gober
Lonnie Graham
Rodney Graham
Renée Green
Richard Haas
Trenton Doyle Hancock
Jenny Holzer
Jim Isermann
Peter Kogler
Roy Lichtenstein
Glenn Ligon
Virgil Marti
Jane Masters
Michael Mercil
Takashi Murakami
Paul Noble
Jorge Pardo
Matthew Ritchie
Francesco Simeti
Kiki Smith
Will Stokes
Do-Ho Suh
Rosemarie Trockel
Andy Warhol
Carrie Mae Weems
William Wegman
Rob Wynne

foreword

JUDITH TANNENBAUM
Richard Brown Baker Curator of Contemporary Art
Museum of Art
Rhode Island School of Design
Providence

Wallpaper has had a checkered past. Highly valued in the eighteenth and nineteenth centuries, by the late twentieth century it had faded into the background or disappeared totally in sophisticated, modernist-inspired American and European homes. Since the 1990s, however, wallpaper seems to be emerging from obscurity. For example, the fashion-savvy interior-design magazine *Wallpaper*, launched in 1996 and geared to "urban modernists and global navigators," took that name to underscore a simple mission: "to live better" through reading it. A recent critically acclaimed exhibition at the Neue Galerie, New York, brought back to light the work of Dagobert Peche (Austrian, 1887–1923), including two dozen spectacular wallpaper designs, and drew attention to the flamboyant and ornamental side of the Wiener Werkstätte (Vienna Workshops), in contrast to the refined, pre-minimalist sensibility normally associated with that early twentieth-century school. In 2001, the Cooper-Hewitt National Design Museum, Smithsonian Institution, New York, mounted a stunning exhibition of historic French scenic wallpapers.

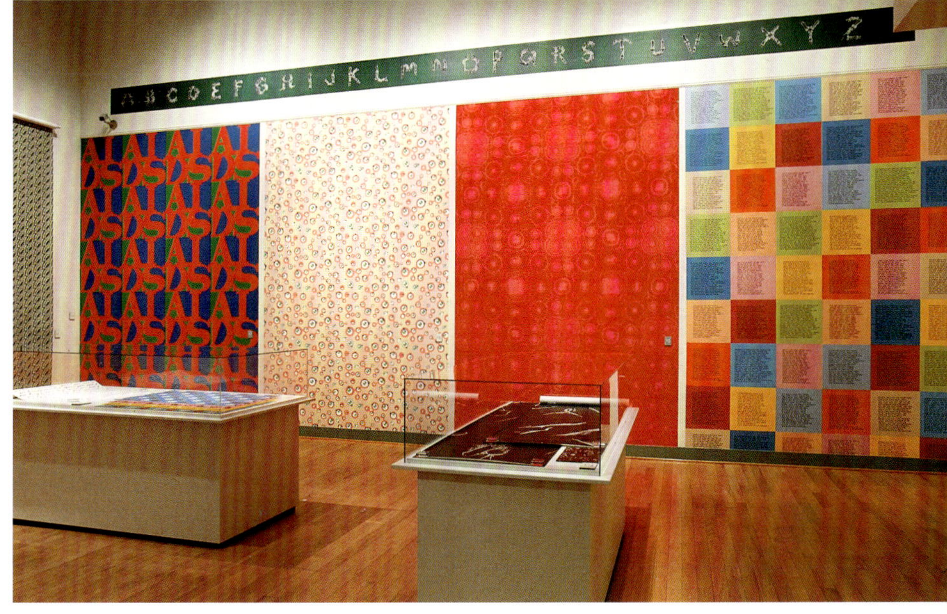

Carrie Mae Weems, General Idea, Takashi Murakami, Jane Masters, Jenny Holzer (walls, l. to r.), and William Wegman (above) at RISD

Over the past decade, I had become increasingly aware of limited-edition wallpapers produced by artists, as opposed to those designed for and distributed to a larger commercial market. For several of these artists, who were trained in painting, sculpture, printmaking, photography, and other fine-art disciplines, it is their primary medium, whereas for others it is a smaller but notable part of their practice. After I came to Rhode Island School of Design (RISD) in 2000 to establish a new department of contemporary art at the Museum, it seemed to be the perfect setting in which to consider this current development and to explore the reasons for and ways in which fine artists are reinventing the traditions of wallpaper. The range of work included in *On the Wall* is remarkable, both for technical innovation and subject matter. What seem at first encounter to be witty, colorful, and upbeat patterns may read upon closer viewing as far more serious and even subversive comments on history and recent socio-political developments.

The exceptional collection of historic wallpapers at the Museum allowed for a concurrent exhibition showing the development of the medium from the eighteenth to the mid-twentieth century.*

Once I began to focus seriously on the topic, it became apparent that this would be a more ambitious exhibition than originally anticipated. The quantity of wall covering we could display and the number of artists we could present, however, would be limited – a selection from a much larger phenomenon. Despite the usual limitations of gallery space and budget, room-sized projects were commissioned from Virgil Marti and Francesco Simeti, and several other large-scale pieces were created specifically for The RISD Museum by Brian Chippendale, Adam Cvijanovic, and Jim Isermann. Included were two Providence-based artists, Chippendale and Jane Masters, who are gaining attention, as well as more than twenty other artists who are recognized nationally and internationally.

The interest and enthusiasm of Marion Boulton Stroud, founder and artistic director of The Fabric Workshop and Museum (who had loaned several works to the RISD exhibition), has enabled us to enlarge the scope of the project. A related exhibition in Philadelphia has been mounted under her direction, and this publication documents both shows. We are most grateful to Ms. Stroud for her expansive vision and generosity and to her staff for their collaboration.

Many of the artists have been directly involved in the exhibition at The RISD Museum. It has been my great joy and honor to work with all of the artists and to see their designs in our galleries and on our walls.

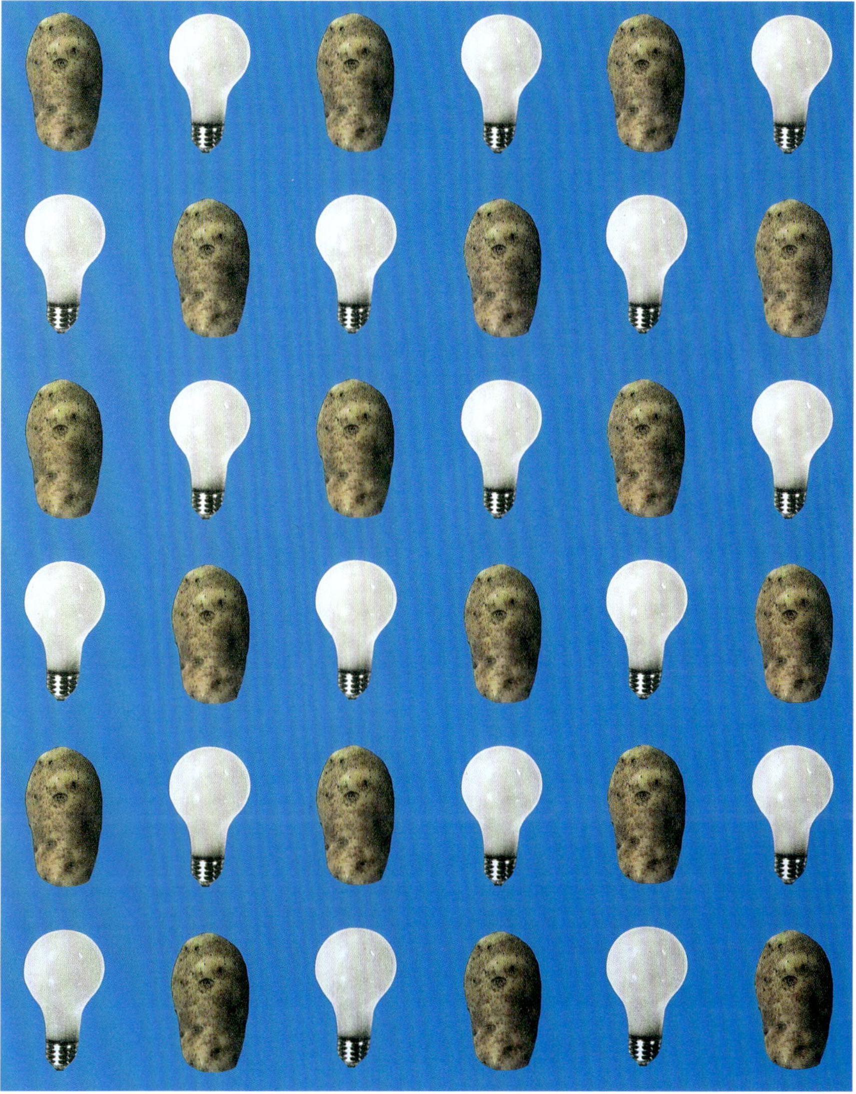

John Baldessari, *Wallpaper for 4 RMS W VU: Potato/Lightbulb – Blue*, 1996, digital color print on paper. Courtesy of the artist and Marian Goodman Gallery, New York

* This exhibition, *Historic Wallpapers, 1750-1949*, was the result of a collaboration between the Department of Decorative Arts at The RISD Museum and participants in a graduate seminar directed by Professor Catherine Wilkinson Zerner, Department of the History of Art and Architecture, Brown University. The seminar was part of a RISD Museum program supported by the Andrew W. Mellon Foundation; the exhibition was supported in part by the Felicia Fund and the Sachem Foundation.

acknowledgements

JUDITH TANNENBAUM
Richard Brown Baker Curator of Contemporary Art
Museum of Art
Rhode Island School of Design
Providence

ELLEN BETHANY NAPIER
Associate Director
The Fabric Workshop and Museum
Philadelphia

During the evolution of the *On the Wall* project at The RISD Museum, many colleagues contributed their expertise and extended themselves with extraordinary good will beyond the usual demands of their jobs. Phillip M. Johnston, former Director, and Lora Urbanelli, Assistant Director and now Interim Director, were supportive from the beginning. Stephen Wing, Head of Installation, and his expert crew seamlessly realized an unusually complex installation. They were complemented by Samuelson/Joyce, who brought long-standing wallpaper-hanging experience to the team; and by the Museum's Paper Technician Linda Catano and Conservator Mimi Leveque. Tara Emsley, Registrar, assisted by Sarah Windham, coordinated shipping arrangements and handling of the artwork. Tracy Jenkins designed the signage and in-house materials; Erik Gould photographed individual works and installation views for the brochure and catalogue with administrative support from Melody Ennis. Special thanks are extended to Judith A. Singsen for editing these publications, and to Elizabeth O'Neil, Head of RISD's Design and Marketing Collaborative, and RISD Assistant Professor Matthew Monk for the design and production supervision of this catalogue and related printed materials.

Thomas A. Michie and Jayne Stokes, Curator and Associate Curator of Decorative Arts at the Museum, willingly assisted with Francesco Simeti's and Ann Agee's installations and shared their knowledge of historic wallpaper. Andrew Raftery, RISD's Head of Printmaking, was an invaluable sounding board for both technical and aesthetic aspects of the show almost from its conception. Some of Raftery's students helped to produce Virgil Marti's *Lotus Room* by screenprinting the wallpaper at The Fabric Workshop and Museum, fabricating the digital decals and labels, and installing the wallpaper with the artist.

Lastly, we are grateful to the Bafflin Foundation and Adler's, both of which provided significant support for the project in Providence.

Tracing the evolution of the *On the Wall* project to its progenitor, our thanks is due above all to Judith Tannenbaum, Richard Brown Baker Curator of Contemporary Art at The RISD Museum, whose conception for the Providence exhibition provided the impetus for our own presentation. Judith has been a patient and insightful interlocutor from beginning to end, and her generosity in allowing us to interpret her ideas has yielded a rich curatorial dialogue.

On the Wall at The Fabric Workshop and Museum (FWM) is also indebted to several curators whose work has propelled wallpaper to the foreground in the last several years. In 1997, Donna De Salvo, now Senior Curator at the Tate Gallery of Modern Art, London, organized the groundbreaking exhibition *Apocalyptic Wallpaper* at the Wexner Center, Ohio, among the first to explore wallpaper beyond the confines of mere decoration and to map the cultural and conceptual stakes of this overlooked practice. In a similar vein, the exemplary work of Kathryn Hiesinger (Curator of European Decorative Arts after 1700, Philadelphia Museum of Art) and Thomas Sokolowski (Director of the Andy Warhol

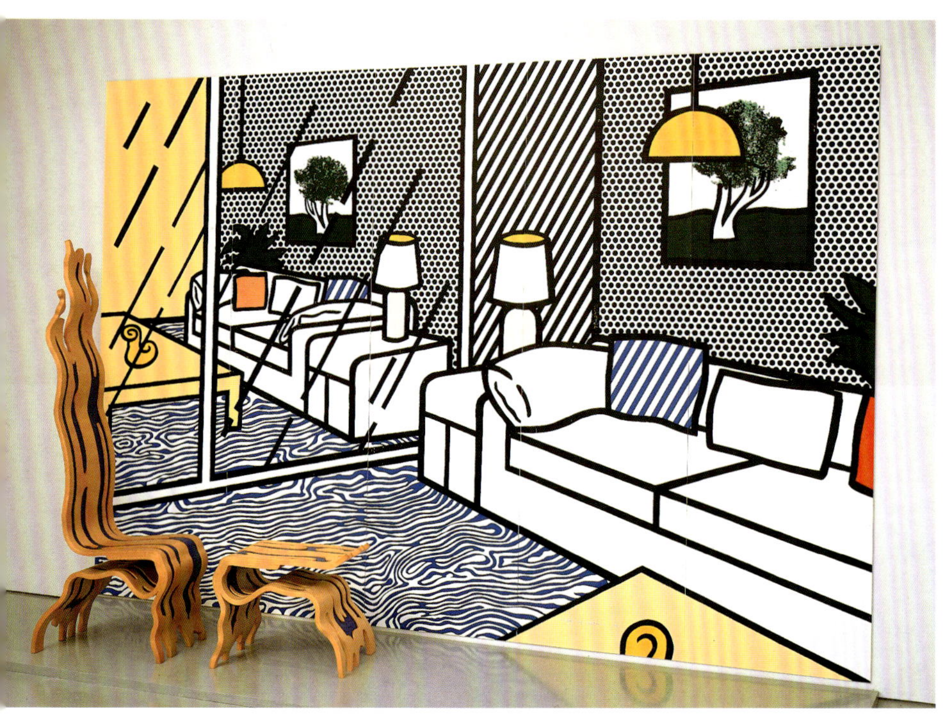

Roy Lichtenstein at FWM, *Interior with Blue Floor* (wallpaper), 1992, hand screenprint on paper. Collection of The RISD Museum; and *Brushstroke Chair and Ottoman*, 1986–89, painted wood. Courtesy of the Estate of Roy Lichtenstein

Museum, Pittsburgh) has yielded invaluable contextual support for the present exhibition. We have supplemented our exhibition with a selection of period wallpapers from the Philadelphia Museum of Art. We are grateful to Anne d'Harnoncourt, George D. Widener Director and C.E.O., and Kathryn Hiesinger at the Philadelphia Museum of Art for making these loans possible.

The FWM would like to extend its most sincere appreciation to all those whose efforts and expertise went into this ambitious undertaking. First and foremost, we recognize Founder/Artistic Director Marion Boulton Stroud, who curated the FWM portion of the exhibition. This show has been in her mind for many years, and she realized the opportunity with extraordinary determination and vision.

We are deeply indebted to the FWM's Artist Advisory Committee, the members of which provided critical suggestions and made us aware of numerous artists who employ this medium. Also at the FWM, Doug Bohr, Director of Exhibitions and Public Programs; Cassandra Coblentz, Curatorial Fellow; and Virgil Marti, Master Printer, tirelessly pursued artists, artworks, and information all over the globe, and conceived and reconceived the gallery installation many times in order to create a space that worked to the advantage of vastly divergent creations. Virgil Marti deserves particular thanks for acting as artist, project coordinator, curator, and advisor – often simultaneously – as he has done for the FWM for two decades. Aaron Igler, Manager of Visual Media and Technology, deserves recognition for his efforts on the production of the publication and for other details related to the exhibition. Janet Samuel, Ursula Ahrens, Matt Suib, Olivia Schreiner, Christina Roberts, and Kate Abercrombie each played a special role in producing and procuring so many complex artworks.

This project could not have been realized without the additional assistance of Doina Adam, Vuyo Baduza, Meg Baird, Tracey Blackman, Blake Bradford, Mary Anne Friel, Thomas Musubi, Sue Patterson, Julie Roat, Julie Shelton Snyder, and Kathryn van Voorhees. Joy Feasley and Paul Swenbeck organized multiple installation teams with their usual grace and dedication. Our thanks go to them, as well as to Carl Allport, George Leaks, James Mason, Nancy Stroud, Peter Tupitza, and Matt Turner, who installed the wallpapers with such precision and care.

Judith A. Singsen, Publications Coordinator and editor at RISD, and Matthew Monk, RISD Assistant Professor and graphic designer, also applied their invaluable talents, dedication, and persistence to this publication on our behalf. We extend our sincere gratitude to Charles F. Stuckey, who provided an essay that examines the conceptual underpinnings and the larger historical practice of artists involved with wallpaper. He has shared his ideas and knowledge with much eloquence. Matt Jolly also played an essential role in shaping the text in this publication, and we admire him greatly for his diligence and critical faculties.

It is our great pleasure to have worked for the first time with Ray Graham and the Board of the Elizabeth Firestone Graham Foundation. We are extremely appreciative of their support of this catalogue and of the work of the emerging and established contemporary artists represented here. As a permanent record, this catalogue is of an importance equal to the exhibitions themselves.

Most of all, the FWM would like to thank all of the artists, from our past collaborators – such as Renée Green, Carrie Mae Weems, and Jorge Pardo – to those who created new works just weeks before the show. We are indebted to Nicole Eisenman, Glenn Ligon, Kiki Smith, and Will Stokes for their sense of adventure and for the lively projects they have produced especially for the Philadelphia exhibition. We are grateful to the other artists-in-residence – Lonnie Graham, Drew Dominick, Viola Frey, Richard Haas, and Michael Mercil – for the works that we are pleased to exhibit in this new context. All of the artists expended enormous effort in making this exhibition a reality, and we must in particular note Mike Bidlo, Adam Cvijanovic, Francesco Simeti, and Rob Wynne for their heroic contributions to the Philadelphia installation.

All of the artists included in the show surmounted challenges in the production of the work and the creation of the respective exhibitions; we thank each of them as individuals for their incredible dedication and vision.

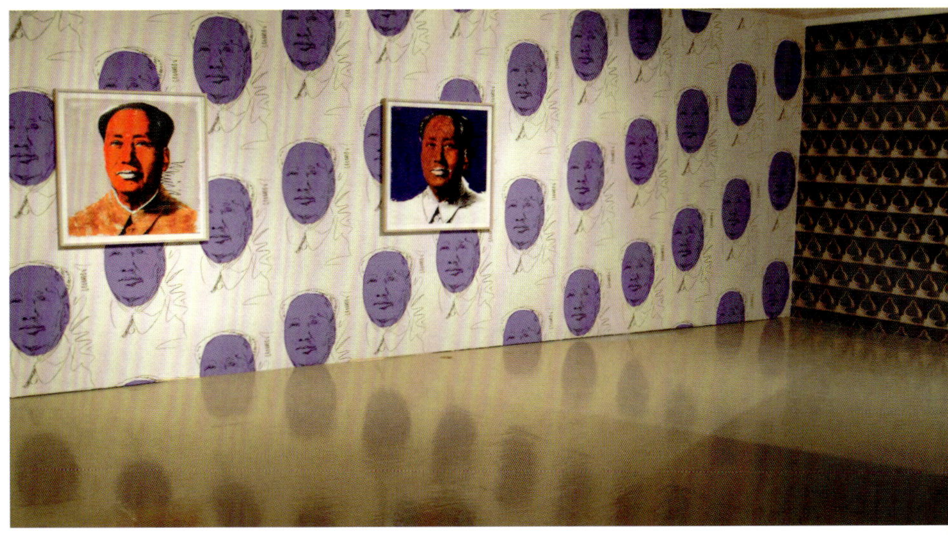

Andy Warhol at FWM, *Mao Wallpaper*, 1974, refabricated for the Andy Warhol Museum, Pittsburgh, 1994, hand screenprint on paper. Courtesy of the Andy Warhol Museum, Pittsburgh; *Mao Tse-Tung*, 1972, hand screenprints on paper in three colorways. Collection of Marion Boulton Stroud. © 2003 Andy Warhol Foundation for the Visual Arts/ARS, New York. Mike Bidlo, *R. Mutt Wallpaper*, 1997/2002, offset print on newsprint. Printed with the assistance of The Fabric Workshop and Museum; courtesy of the artist and Galerie Bruno Bischofberger, Zürich

The RISD Museum and The Fabric Workshop and Museum are grateful to all of the artists and colleagues who made work available for the exhibition. We extend our sincere thanks to the following for their contributions: A/D Gallery, New York; Alexander and Bonin, New York; the Andy Warhol Museum, Pittsburgh; Bellwether Gallery, Brooklyn; CRG Gallery, New York; Cheim & Read, New York; Donald Young Gallery, Chicago; Galerie Bruno Bischofberger, Zurich; Galleria Massimo Minini, Brescia; Anthony Grant; Joseph Holtzman, *nest* magazine, New York, and nest products, New York; James Cohan Gallery, New York; Jenny Holzer Studio, Hoosick (New York); Cassandra Lazano and The Estate of Roy Lichtenstein, New York; Lehmann Maupin Gallery, New York; Marian Goodman Gallery, New York; Marianne Boesky Gallery, New York; Mike Bidlo Studio, New York; Gregory Miller; Nancy Hoffman Gallery, New York; P.P.O.W. Gallery, New York; Philadelphia Museum of Art; Printed Matter, New York; Richard Telles Fine Art, Los Angeles; Robert Gober Studio, New York; Perry Rubenstein and Sara Fitzmaurice; and Tim Gleason Gallery, New York.

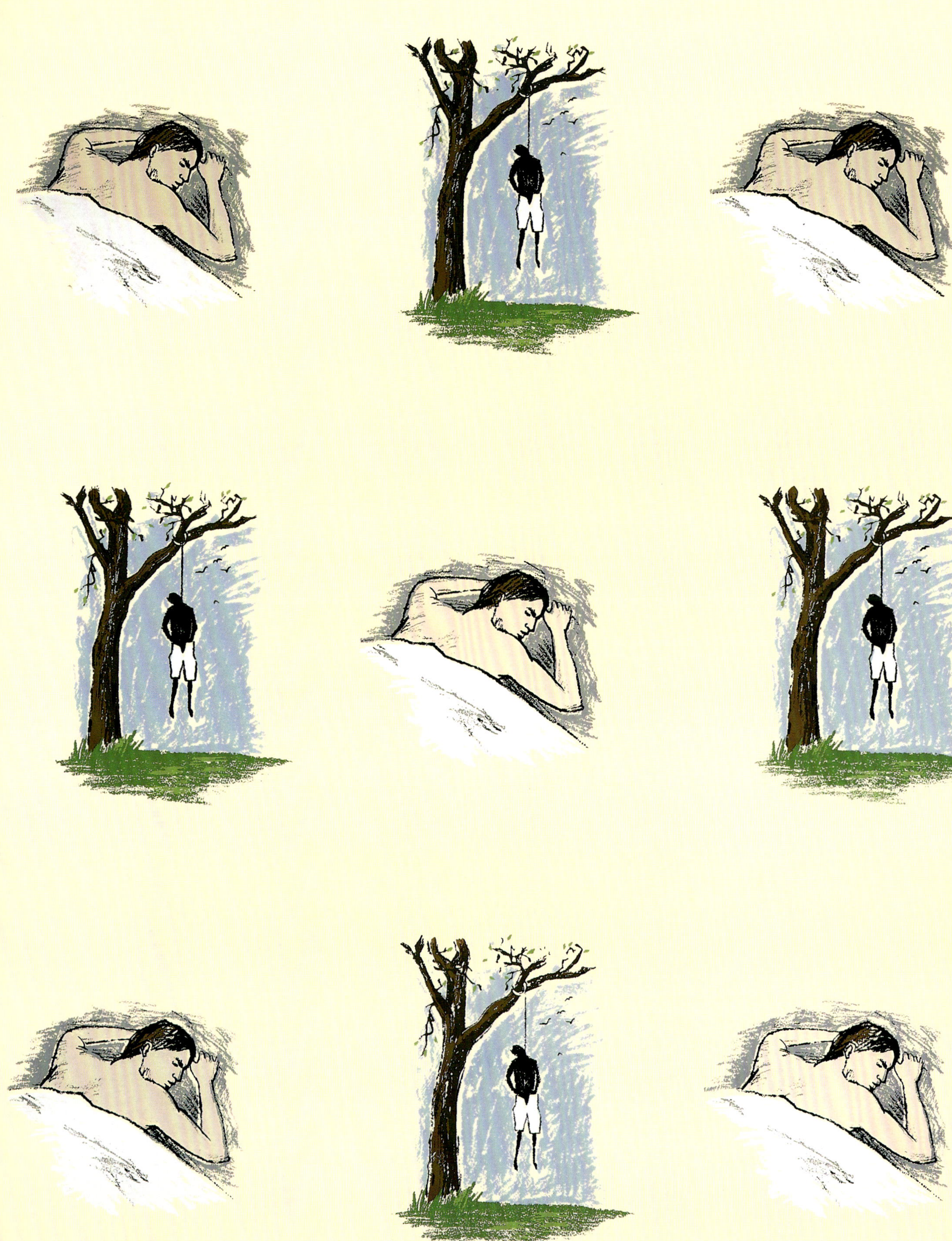

introduction

MARION BOULTON STROUD
Founder/Artistic Director
The Fabric Workshop and Museum
Philadelphia

"Where are we? Who is this? No expression, no attention, no life!
A wallpaper image, imprecise, floating."[1]

FACING PAGE: Robert Gober at FWM, *Hanging Man/Sleeping Man* (wallpaper), 1989, hand screenprint on paper. Collection of Marion Boulton Stroud

BELOW: John Baldessari, *I Will Not Make Any More Boring Art*, 1971/2000, screenprint on paper. Courtesy of the artist and Printed Matter, New York

Could there be a better medium to explore the perennial *pas de deux* between contemporary art and interior design than that of wallpaper? Hand-rendered but earmarked for reproduction, patterned as well as pictorial, *on* the wall but not *of* it, wallpaper clings enigmatically to the conceptual and material margins of architecture, art, and décor. With historical roots in the not-so-fine art of imitation and an unabashed zeal for repetition, wallpaper has been imprinted with the most banal connotations: a needless ornament; a field of pure distraction; in a word, homely. Poised to recede from the visual field should a more deserving object catch our eye, wallpaper from the first has been relegated to the aesthetic background. Clement Greenberg put it quite succinctly on the eve of a Jackson Pollock exhibition. Amateurs, Greenberg opined, were liable to see Pollock's all-over paintings as "nothing but wallpaper."[2]

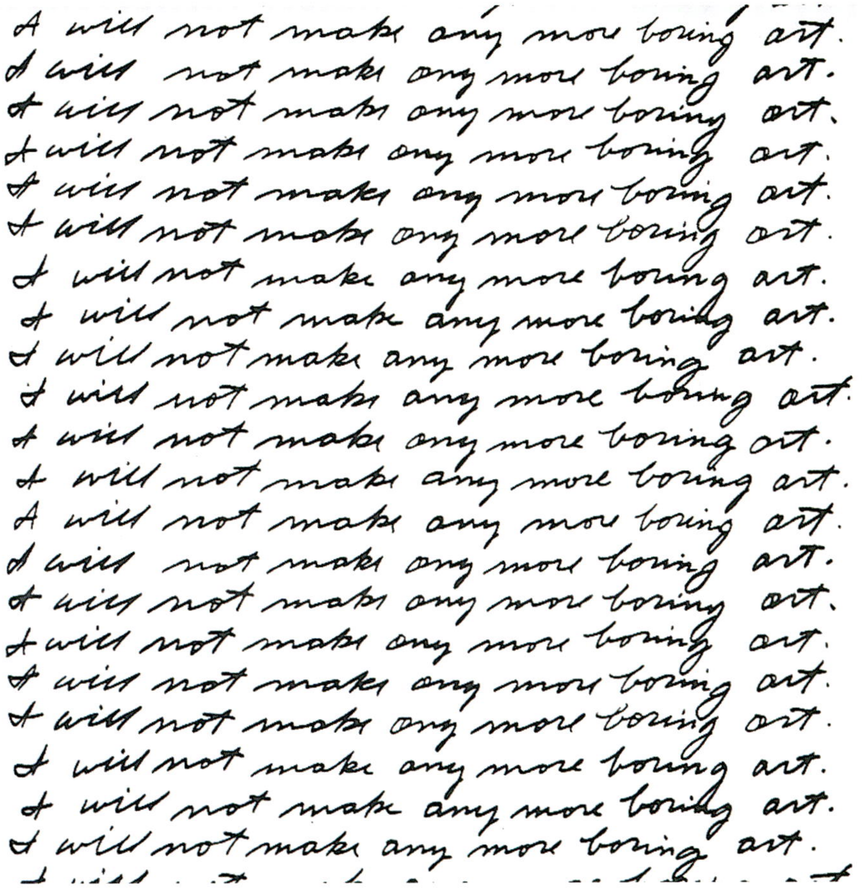

Despite these connotations, or perhaps because of them, a handful of artists working at the intersection of painting, textiles, and installation art have recently taken to pasting paper on museum and gallery walls. They are hardly the first to do so, but their hand-painted, screenprinted, and computer-generated designs suggest that wallpaper is anything but faded.

On the Wall, a collaborative exhibition presented by the Museum of Art, Rhode Island School of Design (RISD), and The Fabric Workshop and Museum (FWM), explores this hybrid practice with a selection of over fifty limited-edition wallpapers by contemporary artists. Working "against the grain," these artists infuse surfaces with alterna-

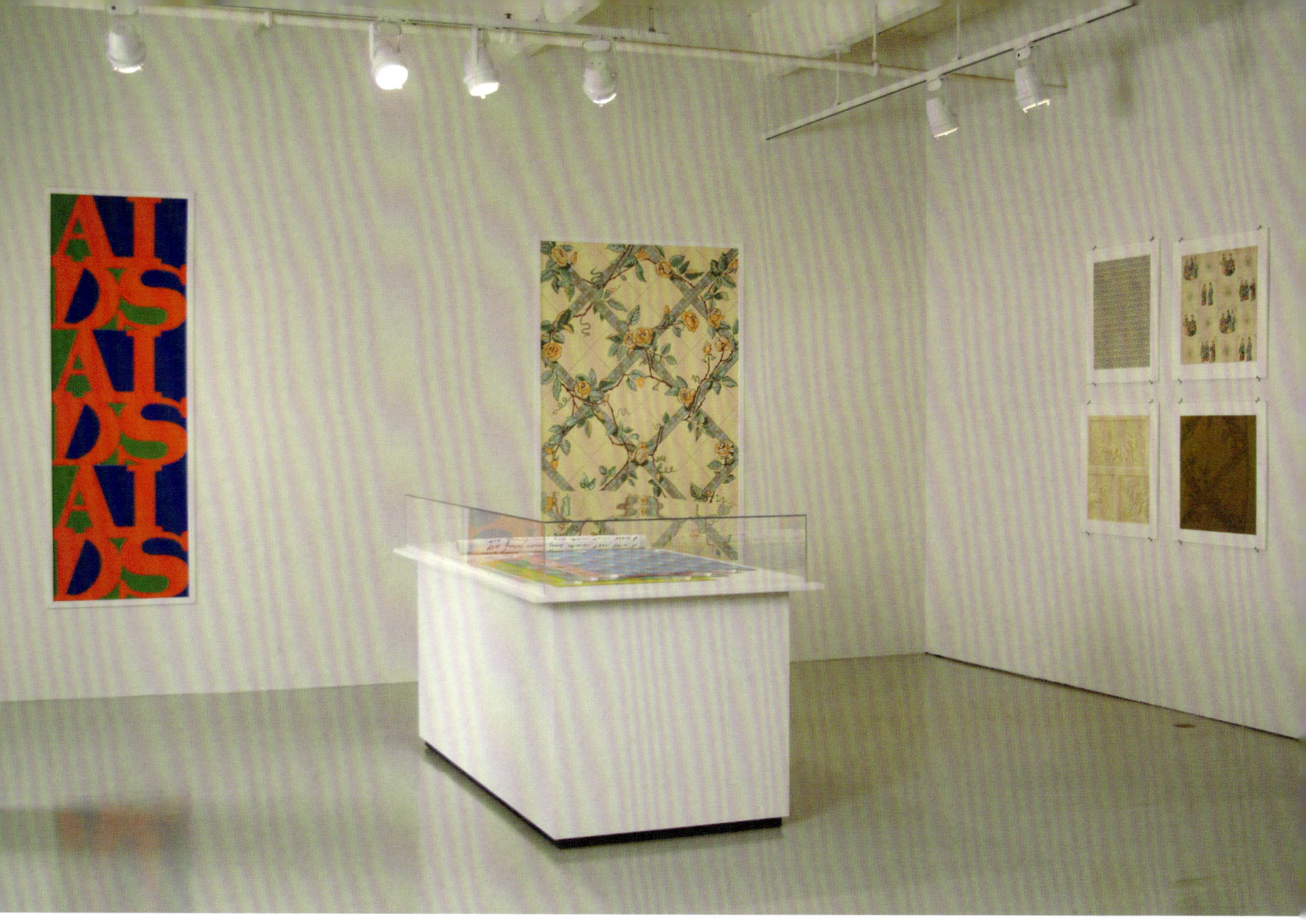

General Idea, Richard Haas, and four historic wallpapers from the Philadelphia Museum of Art (l. to r.), and John Baldessari (in case), at FWM

tive materials and conceptual concerns, broaching a new grammar of design in the process. An exhibition of artist-designed wallpapers provides an ideal occasion for RISD and the FWM to collaborate. Both institutions have nourished the integration of industrial design techniques and contemporary art practices in their own distinct ways, the former in a pedagogical capacity, the latter as a laboratory for artistic experimentation. Indeed, for the FWM, wallpaper evinces strong affiliations with our institutional heritage and aesthetic imagination. Of the thirty-nine artists exhibited in the Providence and Philadelphia shows, seventeen have collaborated with the FWM through our Artist-in-Residence Program. For a quarter century, this collaborative exploration of new materials and repeat design has pointed the way to alternative art practices and counter-histories of contemporary art. The convergence of these techniques is nowhere more evident than in the work of a new international generation of artists fashioning wallpaper with synthetic materials like vinyl, Mylar, foil, and metallic pigments, and utilizing high-speed flexographic and photogravure printing techniques.

Artists have designed wallpapers for centuries, but a history of wallpaper does not unfold discretely nor does it always lie flush. From the first, wallpaper has been intimately linked to questions of aesthetic taste and prevailing attitudes about domestic life and technology. A brief genealogy of wallpaper since the modern era attests to its protean character. Hailed by proponents of Art Nouveau in the middle and late nineteenth century for fusing the fine and decorative arts, wallpaper emerged for British designer-aesthete William Morris as the leitmotif of the decorative schema and an emblem of domestic felicity. "Whatever you have in your rooms," Morris advised, "think first of the walls for they are that which makes your house and home...."[3]

This privilege, however, accorded to wallpaper and to décor in general would quickly be repealed. In the early decades of the twentieth century, the streamlined imperatives of modernist architecture hardened into a disapproval of all things ornamental. In his polemical 1908 manifesto, *Ornament and Crime*, the Viennese architect Adolf Loos disparaged the decorative impulse, likening it, as his title suggests, to a kind of aesthetic felony. Loos's metaphor is indeed telling: a child smearing a pristine white wall.

In the pre-war avant-garde, the déclassé status of wallpaper was pressed into subversive service time and again in the Cubist collage. Often peeling, faded, or slightly yellowed, wallpaper appears in these compositions like matter out of place, a tawdry remnant of low-brow pasted culture and a not so subtle affront to Salon prudishness. It was not until the 1960s that the sheer repeatability of wallpaper would be mobilized as a formal challenge to the definition of the art object; this in the midst of an unprecedented proliferation of images, surfaces, and commodities, and at a moment when the full implications of the Duchampian ready-made were emerging for American artists. The artist in question was, of course, Andy Warhol, and in 1966 he exhibited his *Cow Wallpaper* in the Leo Castelli Gallery. Wallpaper, it seemed, would never be quite the same; nor, for that matter, would art.

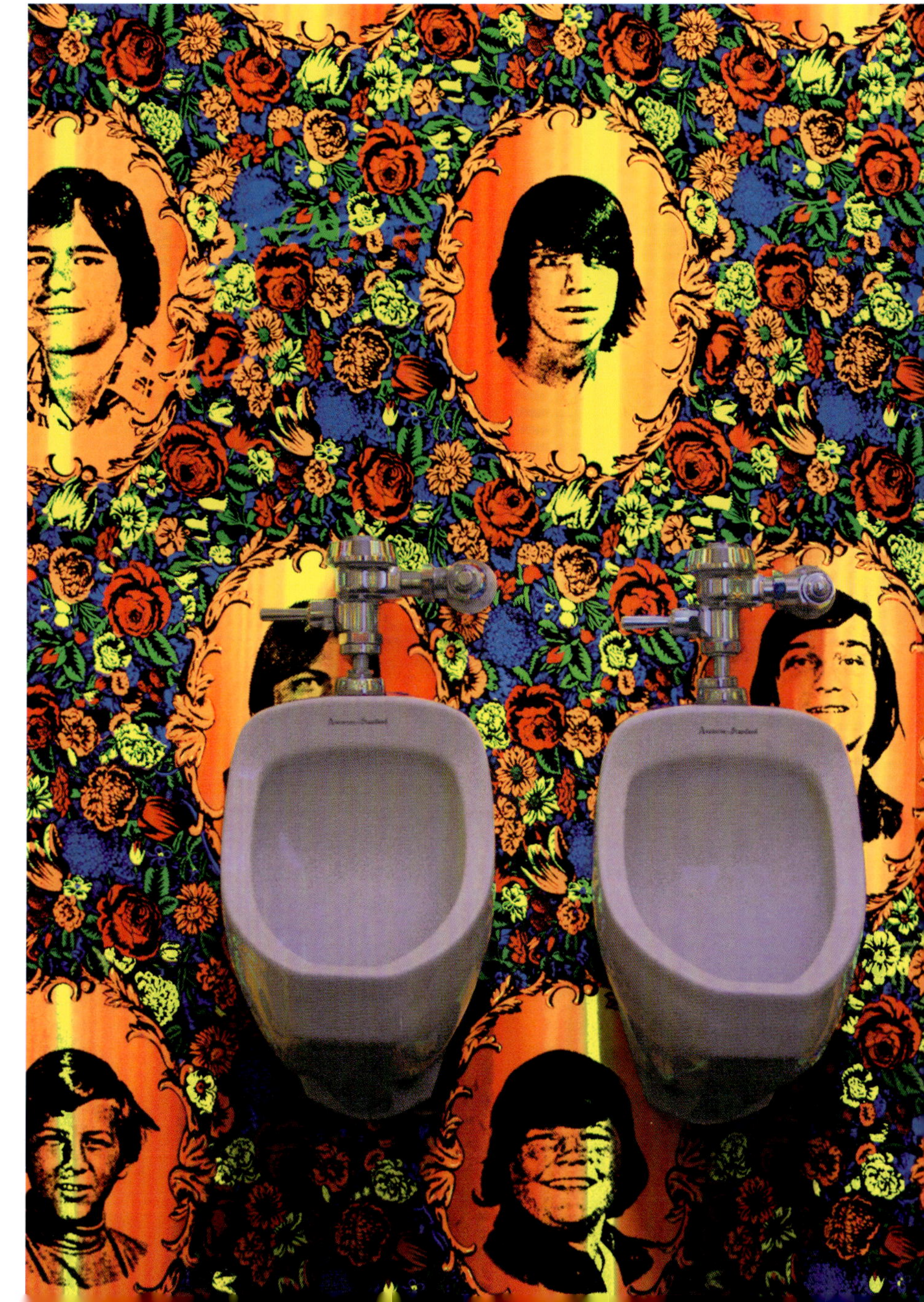

Virgil Marti at FWM, *Bullies* (installation in men's room), 1992/2001, hand screenprint with fluorescent inks and rayon flock on Tyvek (synthetic sheeting) under black light. Collection of The Fabric Workshop and Museum

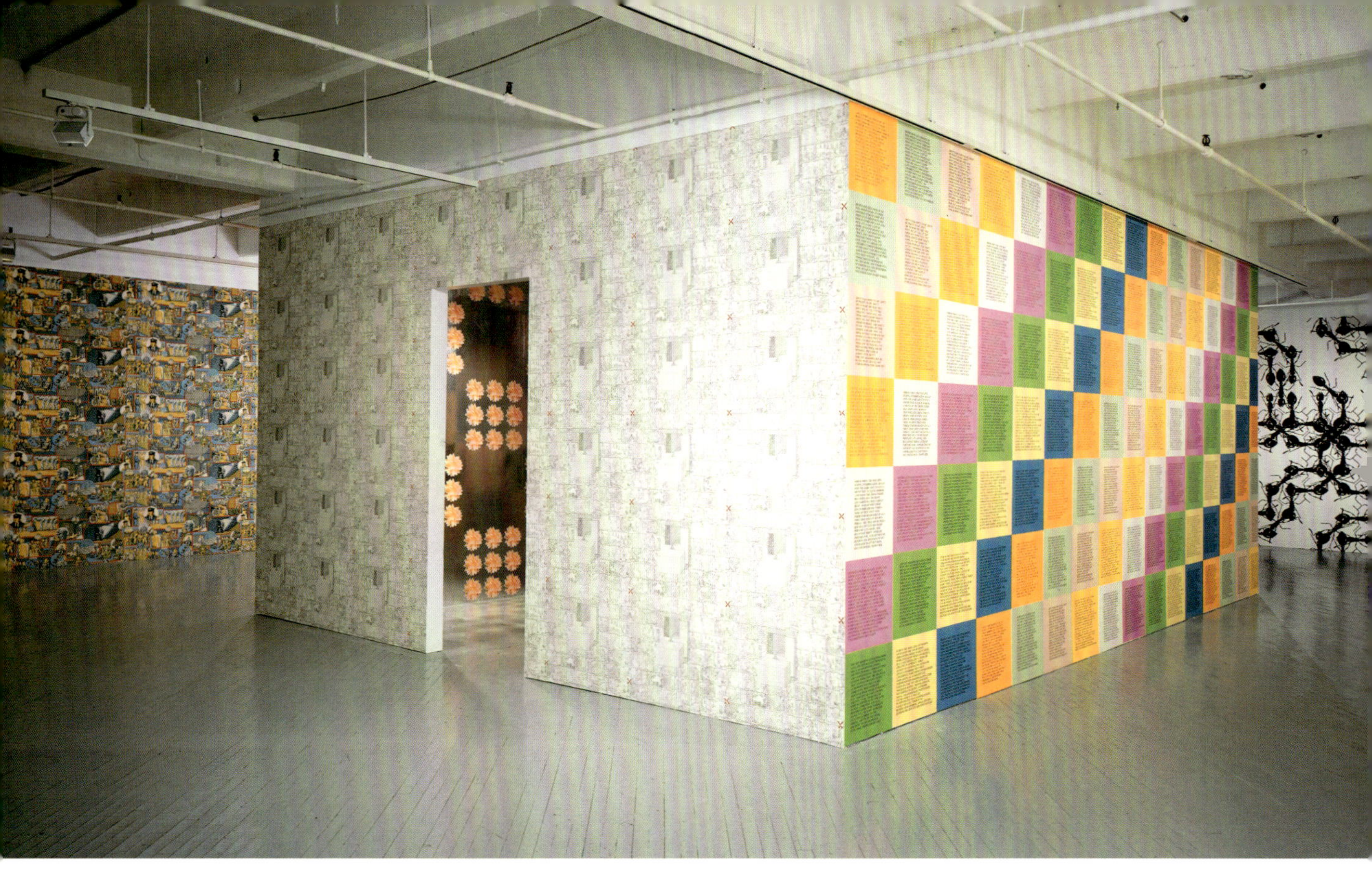

Nicole Eisenman, Paul Noble, Virgil Marti (inside doorway), Jenny Holzer, Peter Kogler (walls, l. to r.), at FWM.

If Warhol posed something of a general proposition about wallpaper's status as art, subsequent generations of artists expanded this investigation in unforeseen ways. Two men in particular have galvanized our interests in pursuing the *On the Wall* project: Virgil Marti and Robert Gober. Marti's experiments with wallpaper alternate between a slightly campy troping of the social and sexual codes of outmoded fashions and cultural ephemera and a more formal investigation of pictorial space and traditional decorative motifs. Often, these conceits overlap in such a way that wallpaper becomes, in Marti's words, something "like the perverted monochrome, where instead of an allover color, you have an allover repeating pattern, and instead of being on a painting chassis [support], it's just directly applied to the wall, so that the architecture becomes the frame."[4] Originally produced and exhibited in 1992, Marti's *Bullies* wallpaper has been installed in the FWM men's lavatory. Mounted under black light, the design repeats yearbook photos of leering adolescent boys across a garish toile pattern. Although not technically site-specific, the darkened space evokes both the proverbial high-school "boy's room" and the ubiquitous black-lit night-club toilet facility, anonymous zones of male aggression and anxiety. Against the background of fluorescent garlands, the threat is gradually defused, and the stares seem to become melancholic, even precious: bullies turned wallflowers.

Robert Gober began experimenting with wallpaper design in the late 1980s and has since produced a series of subtle but often disquieting patterns that subvert the "homely" heritage of the medium. Wallpaper figures into Gober's work as a camouflaged surface that nevertheless operates to pattern our conceptions of self and other. In *Hanging Man/Sleeping Man*, a small drawing of a lynched black man is juxtaposed with one of a sleeping white man, an "image of troubled sleep," in Gober's words. In his *Male and Female Genital Wallpaper* of the same year, sexual identity is simultaneously imposed and dissolved through repetition. Gober's forays into wallpaper are aptly described as "interior decorating with a vengeance" by Dave Hickey,[5] but here the meaning of "interior" slides between its spatial and subjective referents.

Despite the changing forms and reputations of the medium, wallpaper has maintained a relatively straightforward obligation to the wall itself: put simply, to cover it, envelope it, and enliven its mute dimensions. This mandate is precisely what aroused the indignation of high-modernists such as Loos, who felt it degraded the structural integrity of the architectural environment, reducing it to imagistic surface. Questions concerning the relationship between surface and structure have, of course, taken on renewed importance in the last decades with

Renée Green at The Power Plant, Toronto, 1998, *Mise-en-Scène: Commemorative Toile*, 1992; wallpaper: hand screenprint on paper-backed cotton sateen; fabric (upholstery and drapery): hand screenprint on cotton sateen. Created in collaboration with The Fabric Workshop and Museum. Collection of The Fabric Workshop and Museum

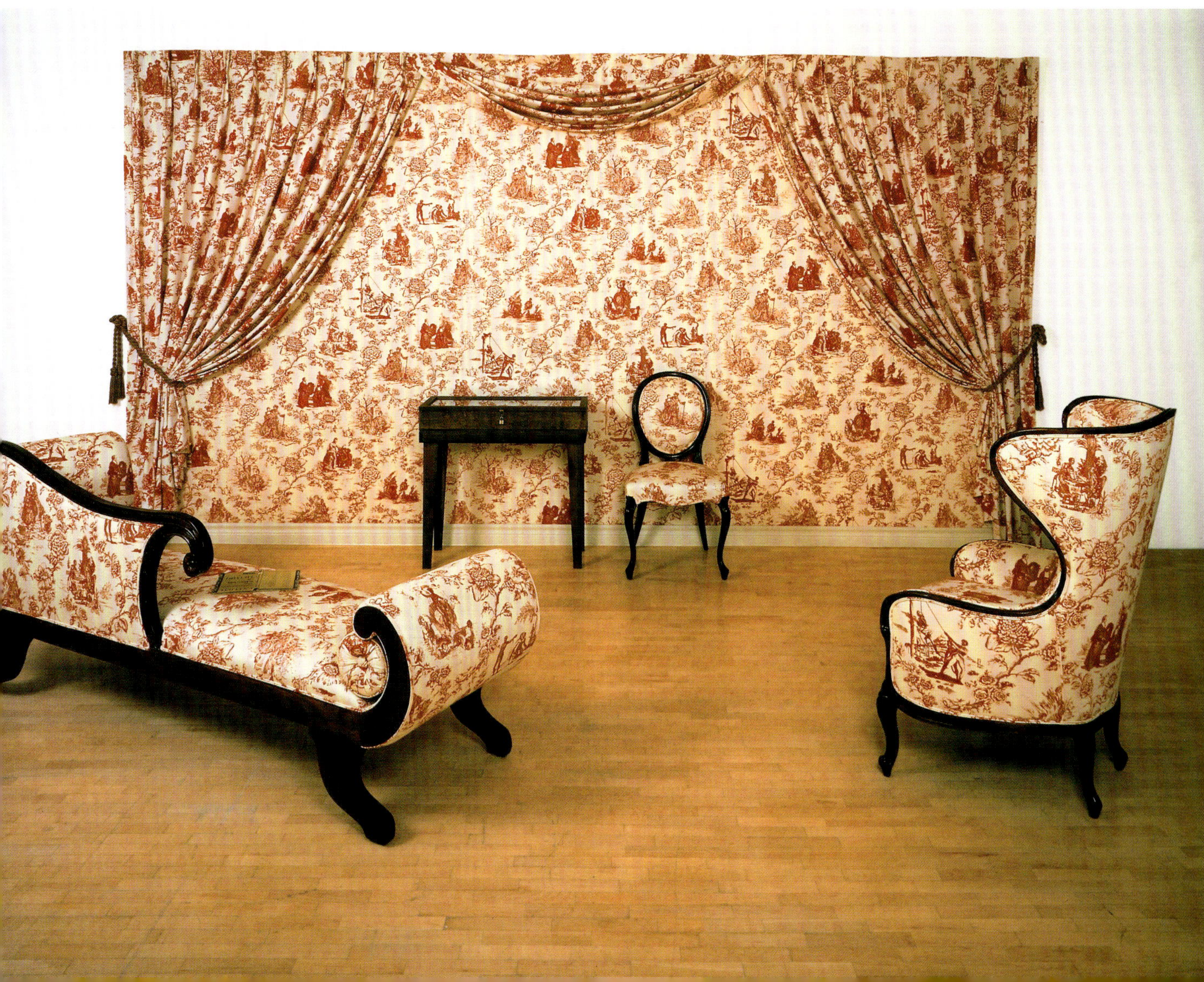

the rise of digital design, projected images, and installation art. Several artists in this exhibition tend to enunciate, rather than obfuscate, the physical parameters of the gallery. Jim Isermann's *Vega*, 1999, for example, is a meticulous assemblage of thermal die-cut vinyl "decals" that incorporate the wall surface itself into the overall pattern by exposing it in the cut-outs of the decals. Bright bands of red and yellow vinyl leave squares, rectangles, and diamonds of bare white wall at their edges. In this spare but insoucient design, which recalls both the concave geometries of post-war American design and the saturated color of 1970s supergraphics, the wall itself seems to oscillate between figure and ground (ill. p. 47).

Peter Kogler's 1992 paper mediates the gallery architecture in a more figurative vein, imaging a network of bulbous black ants crisscrossing the walls and sections of the ceiling. Resolutely flat, the paper spreads vertically along the gallery wall and unexpectedly curls under the ceiling of the archway. Viewed from afar, the ant modules shed their contours and recede into vertical and horizontal vectors, but in another way, the ants, like Kogler's favored industrial piping motif, seem to conjure the invisible "insides" of the wall: plumbing, electrical ducts, wires, support beams, and even the silent traffic of innumerable bugs.

During the heyday of Art Nouveau, wallpaper was often conceived as one complimentary component within a larger decorative motif: a *gesamtkunstwerk* ("total work" of the arts and crafts). In an effort to approach wallpaper's heritage and its resonance with the current trend toward installation art, Viola Frey, Renée Green, Trenton Doyle Hancock, Glenn Ligon, Carrie Mae Weems, and Rob Wynne have integrated their printed papers into larger three-dimensional tableaux comprised of sculptural objects, paintings, and upholstered furniture. Historical examples have in part provided the glue for the *On the Wall* project and have found their way onto the walls in both Providence and Philadelphia. Warhol's *Cow Wallpaper* adorns the entryway to both The RISD Museum and to the FWM sixth-floor gallery. In Philadelphia, Duchamp is represented in absentia by Mike Bidlo's *R. Mutt Wallpaper*, 1997/2002, with its hundreds of black-and-white photocopies of the infamous urinal, confirming the ready-made's enduring shelf-life.

Far earlier samples have also been included at both venues. The RISD Museum has drawn from its own collection, and the FWM has been fortunate to have borrowed material from the Philadelphia Museum of Art.

Ultimately, such a project can only begin to consider the broad-ranging and diverse wallpapers being made by contemporary artists today. Any selection can only act as an invitation to others to pose and attempt to answer the many questions that these artists have so brilliantly and vibrantly raised. Nevertheless, it is our great pleasure to present these installations as they were intended – adhered to

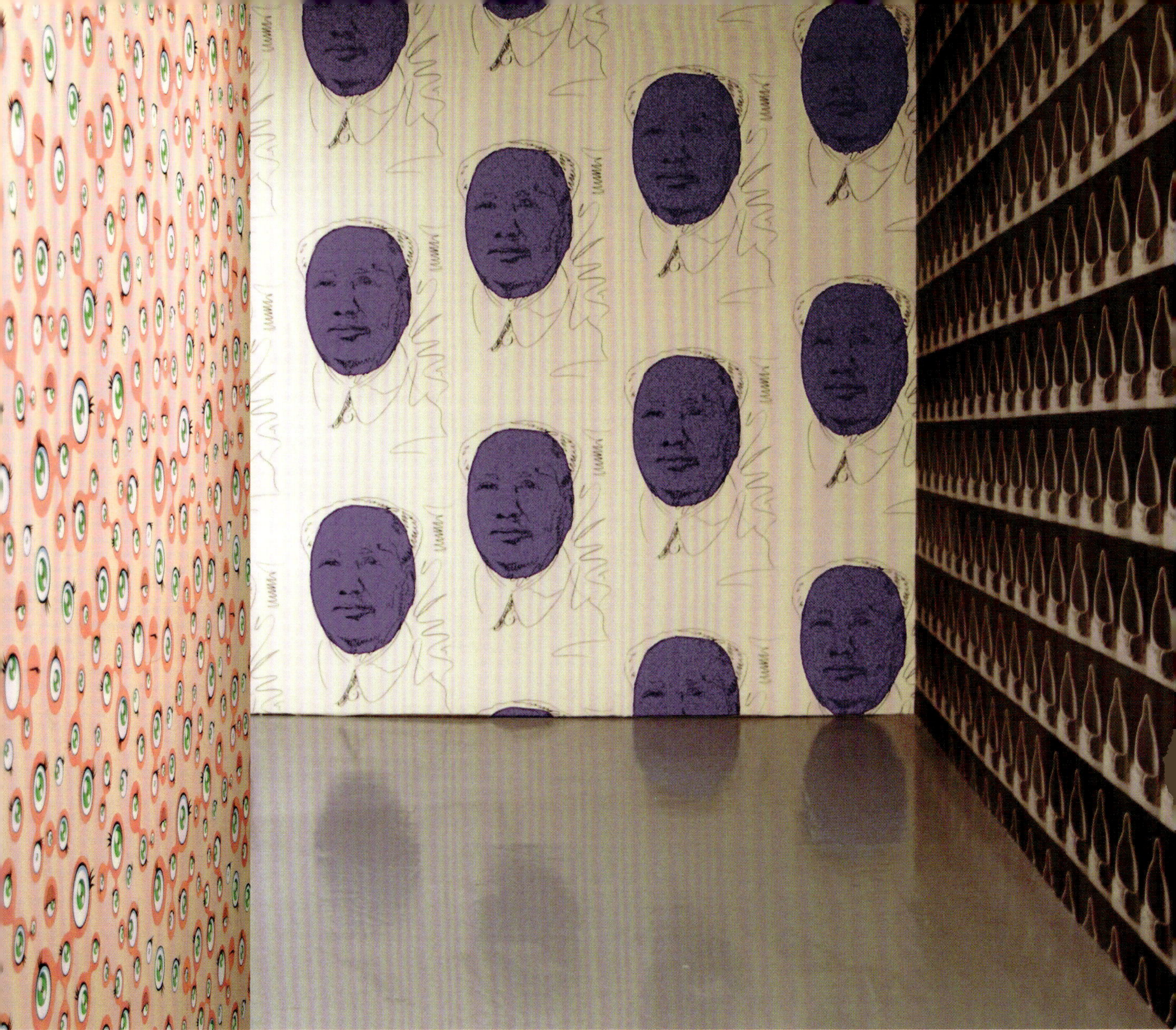

Takashi Murakami, Andy Warhol, and Mike Bidlo (l. to r.) at FWM

walls in particular spaces. As a lasting record of the innovative work of artists and curators, this catalogue is much more than a supplement to the RISD and FWM exhibitions. What goes up (on the wall), of course, must come down, and wallpaper, by its very nature, is an ephemeral art object destined for dereliction. We hope this catalogue will provide something of an afterlife: off the wall, perhaps, but indelibly captured *on the page*. *On the Wall* exemplifies our engagement in investing history and tradition with originality and freshness through the creation of new art.

1 André Fontainas, Review of Henri Matisse in "Le Salon d'Automne," *L'Art moderne* (October 1910), pp. 329–30; cited in Marilyn Oliver Hapgood, *Wallpaper and the Artist: From Dürer to Warhol*. New York: 1992, p. 232. Hapgood's book and Hal Foster's *Design and Crime* (London: 2002) have been key resources for this introduction.

2 Quoted in W.J.T. Mitchell, "Ut Pictora Theoria," *Critical Inquiry* 15 (Winter 1989), p. 366.

3 Cited in *Apocalyptic Wallpaper: Robert Gober, Abigail Lane, Virgil Marti, and Andy Warhol*. Columbus: 1997, p. 33.

4 Interview with the artist at The Fabric Workshop and Museum, Philadelphia, April 2003.

5 In *Robert Gober*. New York: 1993, p. 43.

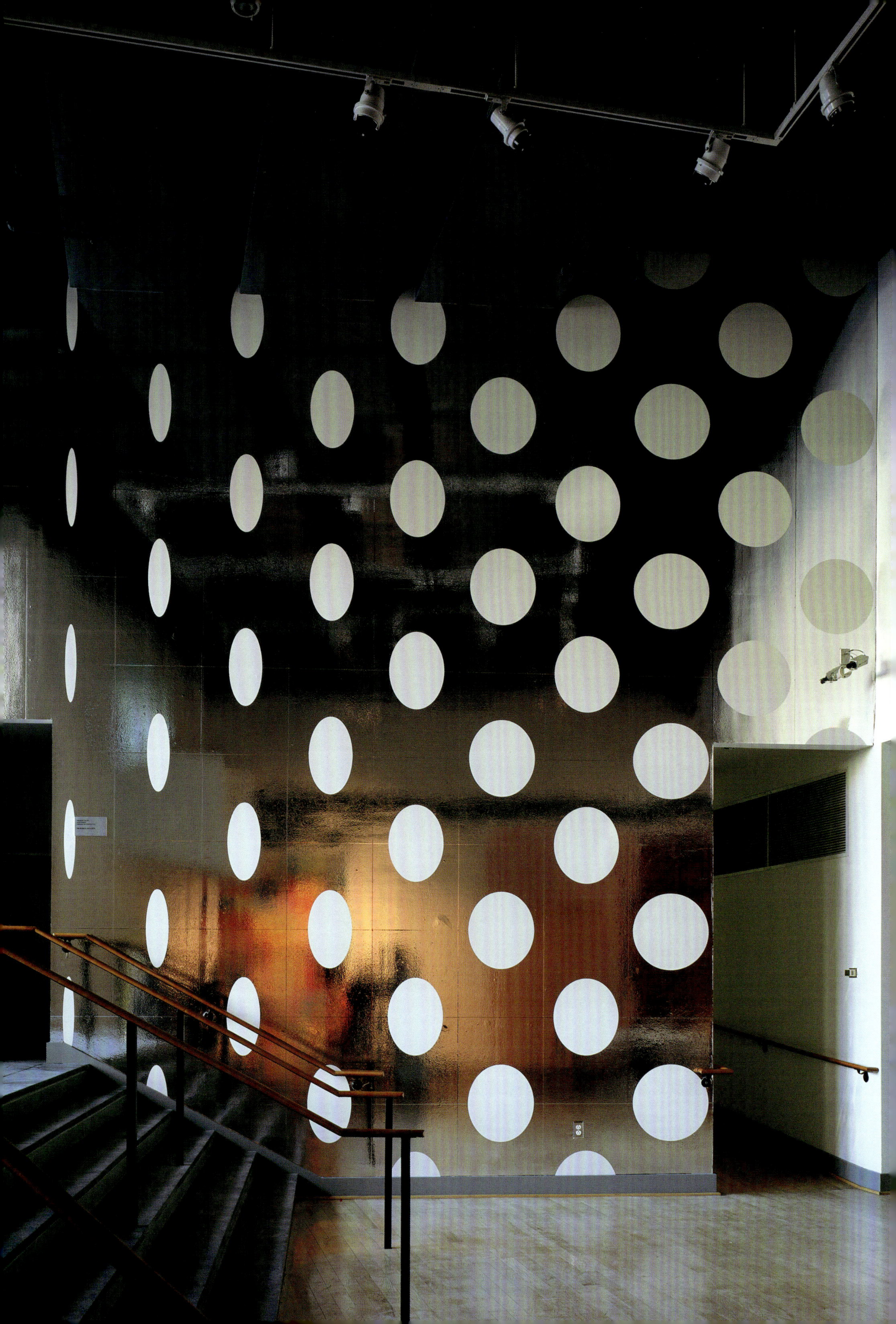

JUDITH TANNENBAUM
Richard Brown Baker Curator of Contemporary Art
Museum of Art
Rhode Island School of Design
Providence

on the wall
wallpaper by contemporary artists

Wallpaper was once ubiquitous and is still common in domestic settings, but it has rarely been given the same kind of attention bestowed on fine-art objects or other applied arts. Nonetheless, many artists – from Albrecht Dürer (1471-1528) to William Morris (1834-96) and Andy Warhol (1928-87) – have created wallpaper and considered this activity to be a significant endeavor.[1]

Despite the move away from ornamentation over the past century in both the fine and applied arts, a number of artists trained as painters, sculptors, and post-modern conceptualists seem to find in wallpaper design an opportunity to return to recognizable imagery and content. How ironic that as the status and popularity of commercially produced wallpaper declined during the twentieth century and the taste for neutral grounds grew, fine artists have come to find the possibilities of wallpaper liberating.

The cross-pollination of design and art or of functional and nonfunctional forms is a complex topic currently of vital interest to a new multinational generation of artists. It is also at the heart of the mission of Rhode Island School of Design (RISD), which trains students in "drawing, painting, modeling, and designing, that they may successfully apply the principles of art to the requirements of trade and manufacture."[2] RISD's Museum acquires works in all areas of art and design and is home to an important collection of historic wallpaper with particular strength in eighteenth- and nineteenth-century French examples, part of its extensive holdings of European and American decorative arts.

On the Wall presents wallpapers by twenty-three artists: a wide-ranging group of works from Andy Warhol's now-classic *Cow Wallpaper* of 1966 to site-specific installations by Virgil Marti, Francesco Simeti, Adam Cvijanovic, and Brian Chippendale created for The RISD Museum exhibition. This selection is only a partial representation of artists trained in the fine arts who are currently adapting and transforming the traditions of wallpaper. Some take advantage of the latest digital technologies, while others continue to employ screenprinting (in commercial use since the nineteenth century) or the hand painting of earlier Chinese and French papers (eighteenth and early nineteenth centuries). Content ranges from

FACING PAGE: Jim Isermann at RISD, *Untitled (0900)*, 2000, plotter-cut Mylar squares. Courtesy of the artist and Richard Telles Fine Art, Los Angeles

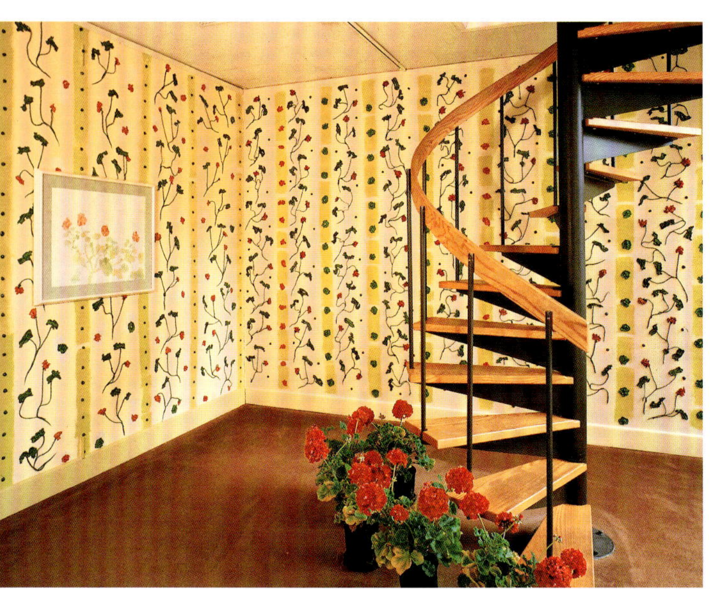

Cynthia Carlson, American, b. 1942, *Richmond, circa 1980*, 1980, room installation (Institute of Contemporary Art, Richmond): walls: acrylic on latex; framed drawing: watercolor on paper; potted geraniums, 10′ x 15′ x 17′ approx. Courtesy of the artist

such current sociopolitical issues as AIDS, race relations, and the recent war in Afghanistan to explorations of architectural space, as well as purely decorative approaches. Precedents include but are not limited to the work of Cynthia Carlson and others associated with the Pattern and Decoration movement of the late 1970s and early 80s. Sol LeWitt and Richard Tuttle have long used the wall itself as a primary element to explore drawing and shape, but their intentions seem radically different.

Repetition – whether of recognizable images or abstract elements – is at the heart of most wallpaper designs; but the use, meaning, and interpretation of repetition may vary from intentional banality, as images recur endlessly, to mindlessness and free association (as elevated by the surrealists), and to even more exalted values associated with mass production as a democratic ideal. Gertrude Stein asserted the positive value of repetition as she simultaneously disavowed its very existence. She posed the question for herself, "Is there repetition or is there insistence? I am inclined to believe that there is no such thing as repetition." Heightening the attention paid to the most basic details of everyday life may sometimes result in miraculous word patterns, such as Stein's deceptively simple "A rose is a rose is a rose...," or in visual statements similarly concise, elegant, and endlessly reproducible. On the other hand, Charlotte Perkins Gilman's unnamed protagonist in *The Yellow Wallpaper*[3] progresses quickly from postpartum depression to full-blown madness when confined day and night to a wallpapered room by her well-meaning physician husband, the "sprawling and flamboyant" patterns her only companion and source of interaction.

Another critical consideration regarding repeat patterns is background versus foreground. Fine artists usually aim to produce objects that are the focus of attention, whether on a museum wall, in a public setting, or in a private home; but wallpaper is not framed or put on a pedestal. It is meant to unify or enliven an environment as just one of a number of elements. The wallpaper designer has a difficult task: to create patterns that are interesting enough to be noticed and to produce the desired ambiance, but that are not so striking as to detract from the furnishings, artworks, and architectural features of a room. Too often, wallpaper becomes the visual equivalent of Muzak, inoffensive but banal as it infiltrates everyday living and work spaces. One exception is the panoramic wallpapers produced by firms such as Zuber and Company (Rixheim, France, 1790-present), which were much sought after during the nineteenth century and to a lesser degree at present. Printed by hand from hundreds – even thousands – of different woodblocks, these

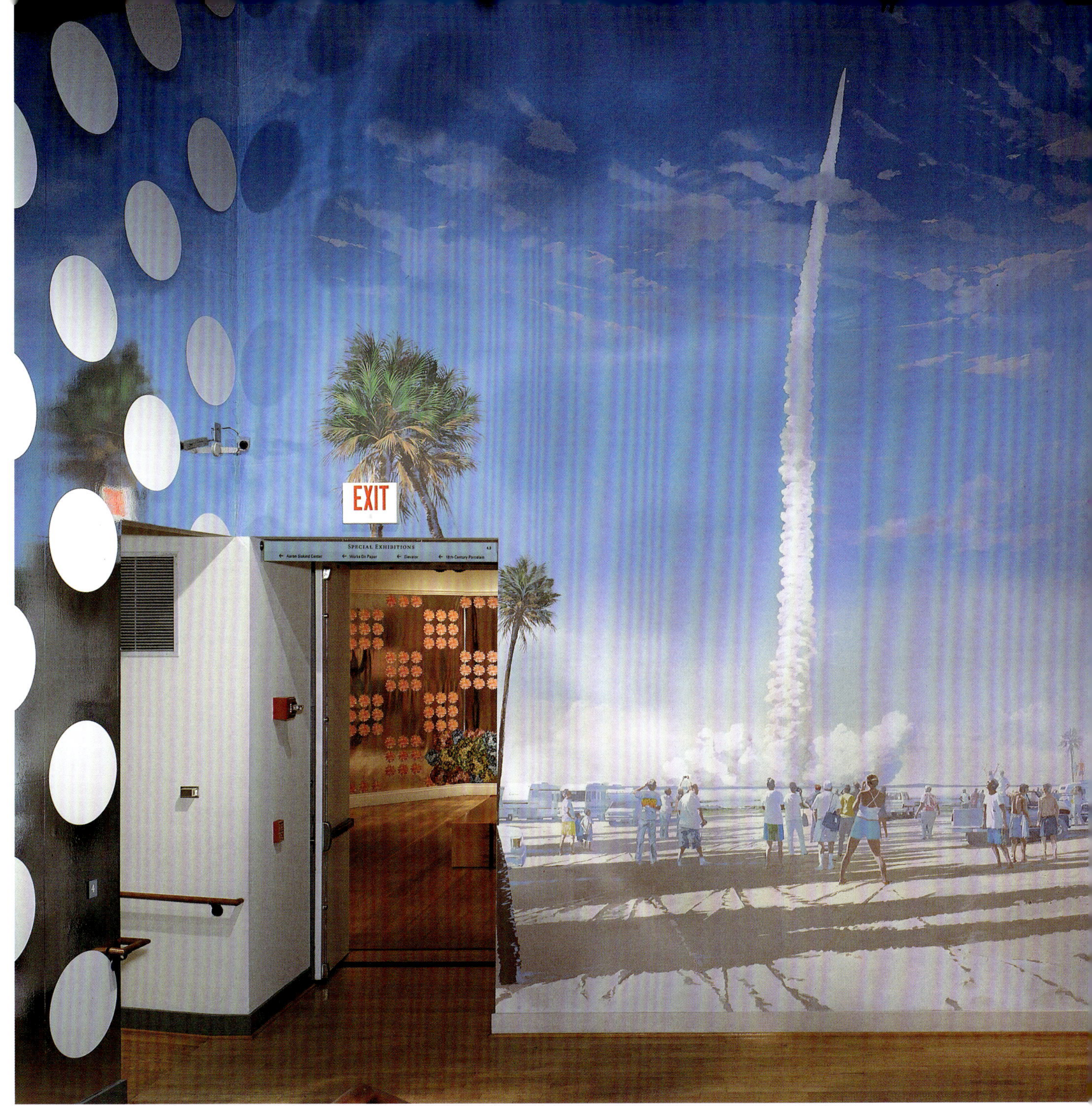

Adam Cvijanovic at RISD, *Space Park*, 2003, Flasche, acrylic, and latex on Tyvek (synthetic sheeting). Courtesy of the artist and Bellwether Gallery, Brooklyn

expansive landscapes reflected the European passion for travel to exotic places from the Far East to the American West and the tropics of Latin America. Executed at great expense for grand houses, they were meant to be the focus of attention, as mural paintings would be.

Adam Cvijanovic's *Space Park*, created for the Providence exhibition, was inspired by Zuber scenic wallpapers. Based on National Air and Space Administration (NASA) photographs but painted by hand in about forty-five colors on Tyvek, a late-twentieth-century material used for building construction as well as mailing envelopes, the work may be removed from the wall for adaptation or reuse at another site. Tourists viewing a Space Shuttle launch (from a waterfront park in Titusville, Florida) with recreational vehicles in the foreground is clearly a contemporary subject, but the tops of palm trees high in the gallery allude to *El Dorado*, one of the most famous nineteenth-century scenic papers

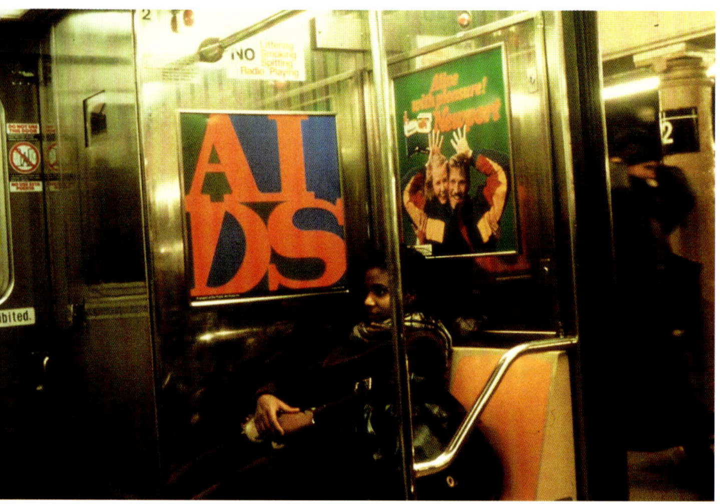

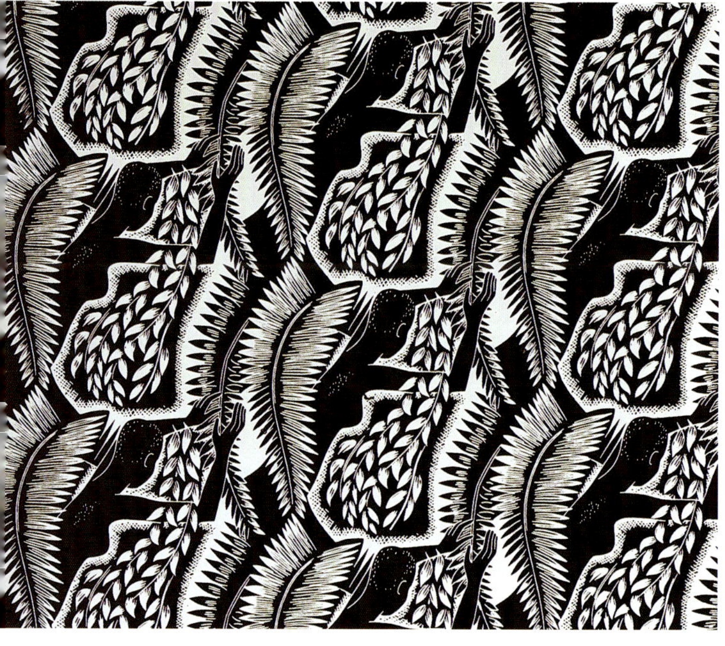

TOP: General Idea, *AIDS Poster Project*, 1989, installed in three thousand New York subway cars. © General Idea Editions. Image courtesy of Blackwood Gallery, University of Toronto, Mississauga, Ontario

ABOVE: Carrie Mae Weems, *Looking High and Low* (wallpaper) from the "Africa Series," 1993, hand screenprint on paper. Courtesy of P.P.O.W. Gallery, New York (at RISD). Collection of The Fabric Workshop and Museum

FACING PAGE: Do-Ho Suh, *Who Am We? (multi)*, 2000, color offset print on paper. Courtesy of the artist and Lehmann Maupin Gallery, New York

(designed ca. 1848).[4] A cloud of exhaust from the rocket connects the earth to infinite space, as Cvijanovic links the daily lives of ordinary observers to expanses of the natural environment. Ironically, the tragic explosion of the Space Shuttle Columbia following reentry occurred just days after the installation of Cvijanovic's work.

When wallpaper is exhibited in a museum or art gallery, it usually comes to the fore rather than remaining in the background. Andy Warhol first presented his iconic *Cow Wallpaper* in 1966 at the Leo Castelli Gallery, New York, without anything else in the room. In 1971, he showed it at the Whitney Museum, New York, as a backdrop (in red on violet instead of the original pink on yellow) for an installation of his own paintings. Appropriating an image that recalls the cow used to advertise Borden's milk in the mid-twentieth century, as well as bovine inhabitants of earlier European landscape paintings, this repeat of seemingly larger-than-life heads "constituted a deadpan attack on the sacred cows of high art and taste" for which "wallpaper – an irredeemably 'popular' art form – was the perfect vehicle."[5] Subsequently, in 1974, Warhol exhibited a large group of his Mao paintings against a wallpaper featuring purple ovals with the Chairman's face on a white ground (ills. pp. 9, 17, 34).

General Idea's red, blue, and green AIDS wallpaper, which is an "infected" version of Robert Indiana's LOVE logo, was originally printed in poster format. The AIDS paper is meant to be installed as a background for the group's other works or to be seen in well-trafficked public spaces, thus underscoring the prevalence of the disease and how it has infiltrated contemporary life. Do-Ho Suh's *Who Am We?*, featuring a grid of tiny faces of the artist's friends and family, is similarly designed as background for his other work. Unlike Warhol and General Idea, whose patterns read loud and clear from a distance, Suh's repeated images require close viewing to discern individual faces rather than an overall pattern that reads as texture. Carrie Mae Weems's *Looking High and Low*, a stylized black-and-white repeat pattern of a female figure enmeshed in a jungle of vines and palm or fern fronds, was created for the gallery walls of an installation that included a large folding screen, photographs, and ceramic plates from the artist's "Africa Series." Weems, who was searching for her own roots in Africa, appropriated this pattern from the endpapers of the first edition of George Bernard Shaw's much read book of 1933, *Adventures of a Black Girl in Her Search for God.*[6]

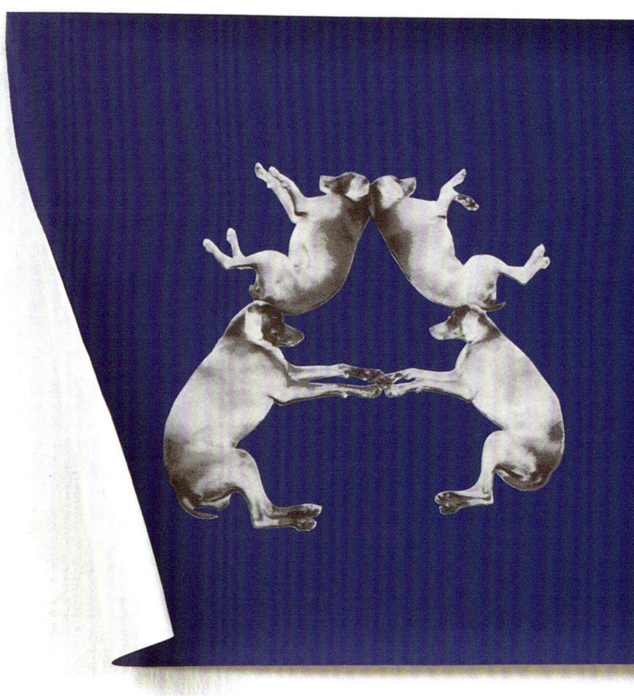

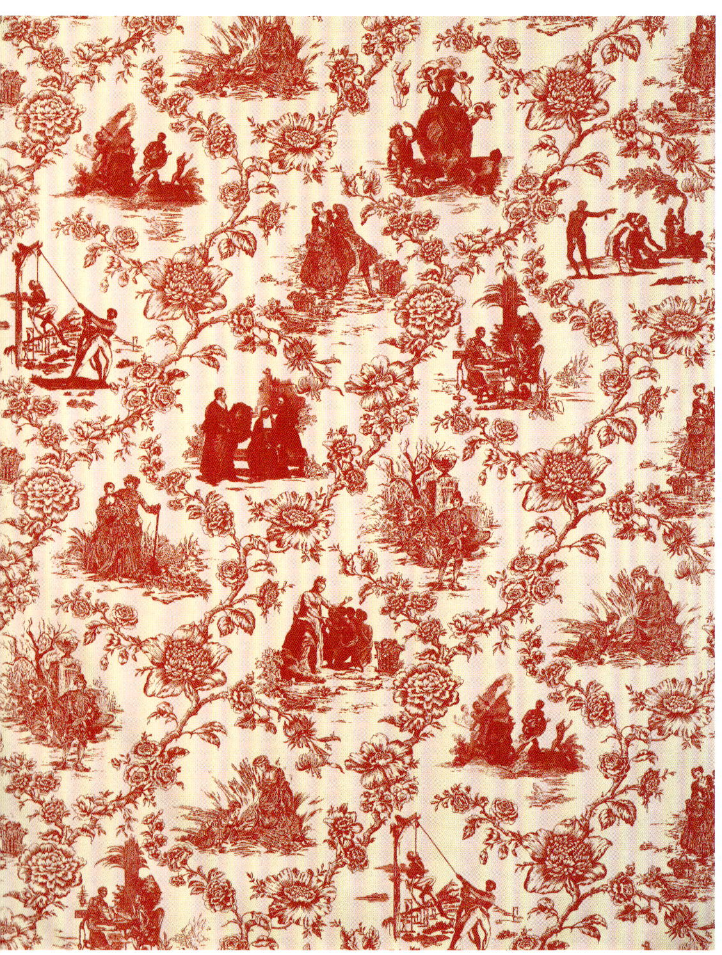

A number of artists in the exhibition look back to historical precedents, but update and/or subvert their content. Renée Green's red-and-white *Mise-en-Scène: Commemorative Toile* employs the two-color format commonly used in France for *toile* (printed cotton fabric) wall coverings from the beginning of the eighteenth century to the present. Amidst allegorical groups of gods and goddesses, pastoral scenes, and floral motifs typical of toiles, but altered in some cases, she inserts historical images of anticolonial uprisings. One of these vignettes was derived from an engraving published in 1805 of the hanging of French officers by the Haitian army of former black slaves during the revolution of ca. 1800–04. The hangings were in retaliation for atrocities committed by the French army. Green thereby makes visible and forces the viewer to confront past events that are all too often disguised, suppressed, and unacknowledged.

Francesco Simeti pursued a similar path in his installation for *On the Wall*. Starting from a late eighteenth-century French wallpaper fragment in The RISD Museum's collection, which features Chinese garden and landscape motifs, he inserted images of Afghani refugees washing clothes in a river and weighed down with bundles as they flee, as well as Afghani men on bicycles holding bunches of balloons to sell during the U.S. intervention in their country. This pattern, entitled *Arabian Nights* (also the title of the entire installation), and a background pattern called *Are You Ready?*, depicting a crowd of refugees surging toward the viewer, were created using recent newspaper photo-

Renée Green, *Mise-en-Scène: Commemorative Toile*, 1992, hand screenprint on paper-backed cotton sateen. Created in collaboration with The Fabric Workshop and Museum. Collection of The Fabric Workshop and Museum

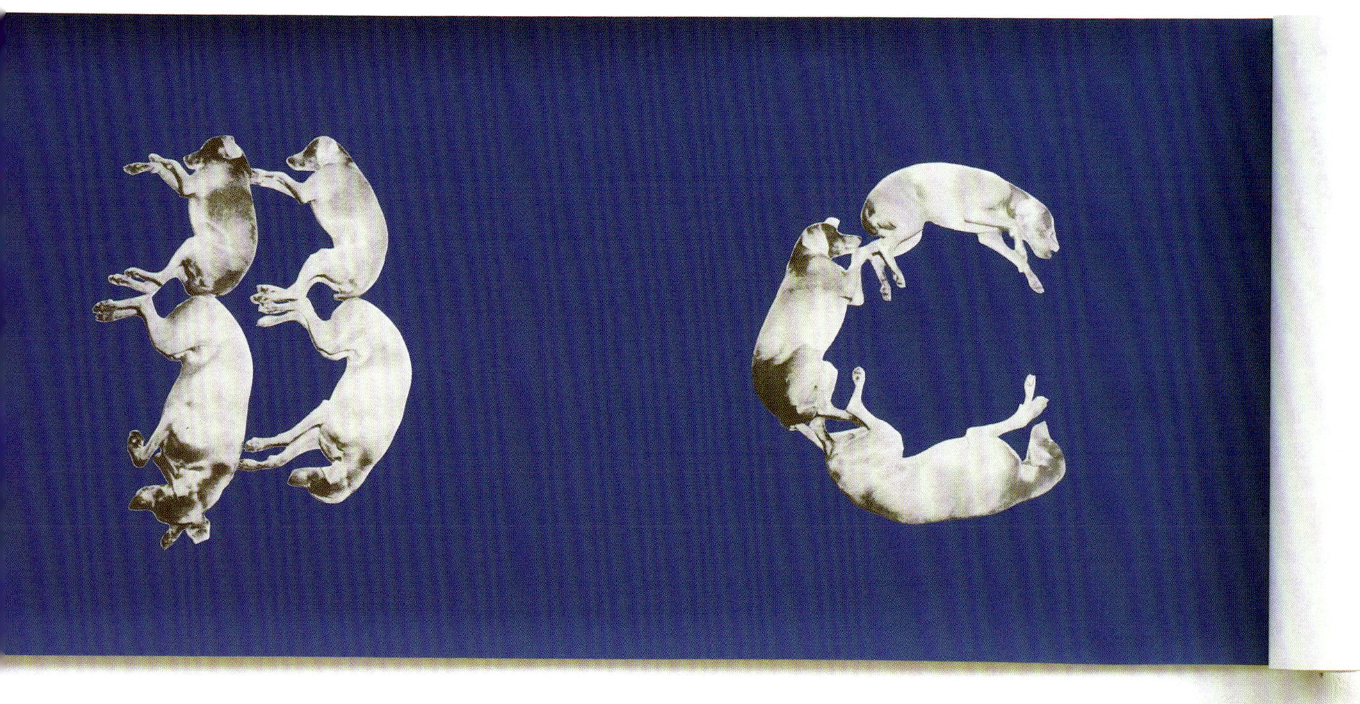

William Wegman, *Alphabet Border*, 1993, hand screenprint on paper. Courtesy of the artist and A/D Gallery, New York

graphs. Simeti subtly interweaves these images so that it is difficult to distinguish a bucolic landscape from a political disaster, thus underscoring how we tend to repress the horrors of war even though the images of displacement and death may be all around us. We see them, but they do not register (ill. inside front cover and p. 50). Simeti, a citizen of both Italy and the U.S., moved to New York in the early 1990s, lived there for seven years, and recently relocated to Sicily. He was struck by how much more removed Americans are from political events than Europeans seem to be. His work changed dramatically during his stay in the U.S. from joyful sculpture to digital work based on environmental and political disasters.[7]

A nineteenth-century lithograph from a French children's book is the source for Rodney Graham's *City Self/Country Self* wallpaper, which was produced and originally shown in conjunction with a video projection of the same name. Graham has transposed his own likeness onto the faces of the two characters in the original print – an urban dandy and a provincial rustic who is being booted in the rear by the city slicker (ill. pp. 51, 55). Although set in Paris in the 1860s, the image recalls the humorous caricatures of eighteenth-century British artist Thomas Rowlandson, known for creating witty watercolors and prints and also wallpaper. William Wegman adapts the format of the traditional wallpaper border, a narrow horizontal band most often affixed high on the wall; but he replaces the usual decorative motifs with a frieze of his well-known Weimaraners playfully contorted to shape the letters of the alphabet from A to Z. Wegman's wallpaper also recalls the English pictorial alphabets designed for children's book illustrations and tableware, popular since the nineteenth century.

Humor and cartoonlike styles characterize the creations of several artists. Takashi Murakami, whose work is steeped in classical Japanese painting as well as in Japanese animation, computer graphics, and Western popular culture, has

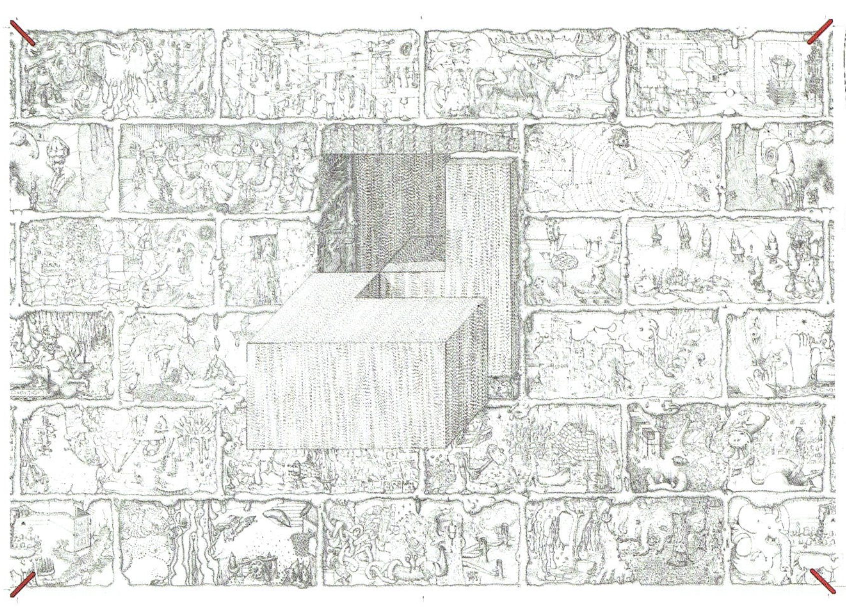

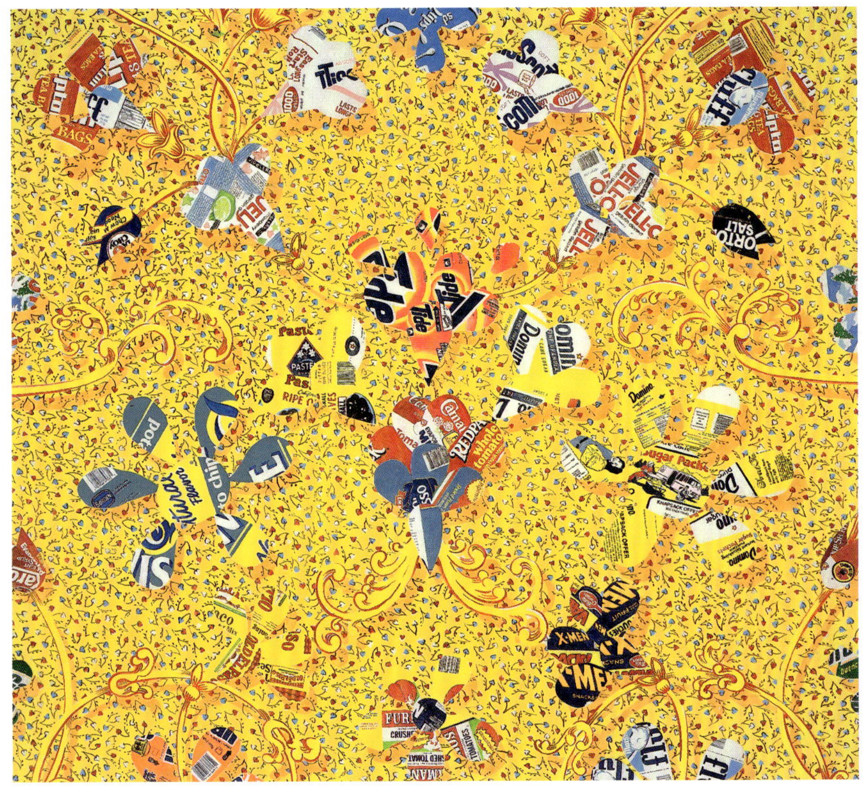

featured his *Jellyfish Eyes* pattern in a series of pink paintings. These green-and-white black-lashed eyes also appear on his anthropomorphized mushroom sculptures and the recurring two-dimensional characters that populate Murakami's fecund fantasy world. In *nobnest zed*, Paul Noble limits his palette to gray and white (with red accents indicating the registration marks at the four corners of each sheet, here used as a compositional element), but upon close examination the gridlike composition teems with activity. Created as a project for *nest* magazine, this wallpaper is related to the London-based artist's series of graphite drawings entitled *Nobson*, a fictitious town where an alphabet of buildings represents various social functions. Strange animals and human figures participate in indescribable activities in architectural and landscape settings that are imaginative and bizarre. Flemish painters Hieronymus Bosch (1462?-1516) and Pieter Breughel the Elder (ca. 1525-69) meet the comic strip.

TOP: Paul Noble, *nobnest zed*, 2002, offset print on paper. Courtesy of *nest* magazine and nest products

ABOVE: Ann Agee at RISD, *Jello Yellow Calico*, 1995, gouache on rice paper. Courtesy of the artist

FACING PAGE: Takashi Murakami, *Jellyfish Eyes*, 2002, hand screenprint on paper. Courtesy of Marianne Boesky Gallery, New York

John Baldessari's humor is rooted in the conceptual. His *I Will Not Make Any More Boring Art* wallpaper resulted from a project at the Nova Scotia College of Art and Design in 1971. He sent a proposal to a class of students there, and in response they wrote these words directly on the walls of a gallery in mimicry of the way pupils have been punished for generations by having to write a sentence repeatedly on the

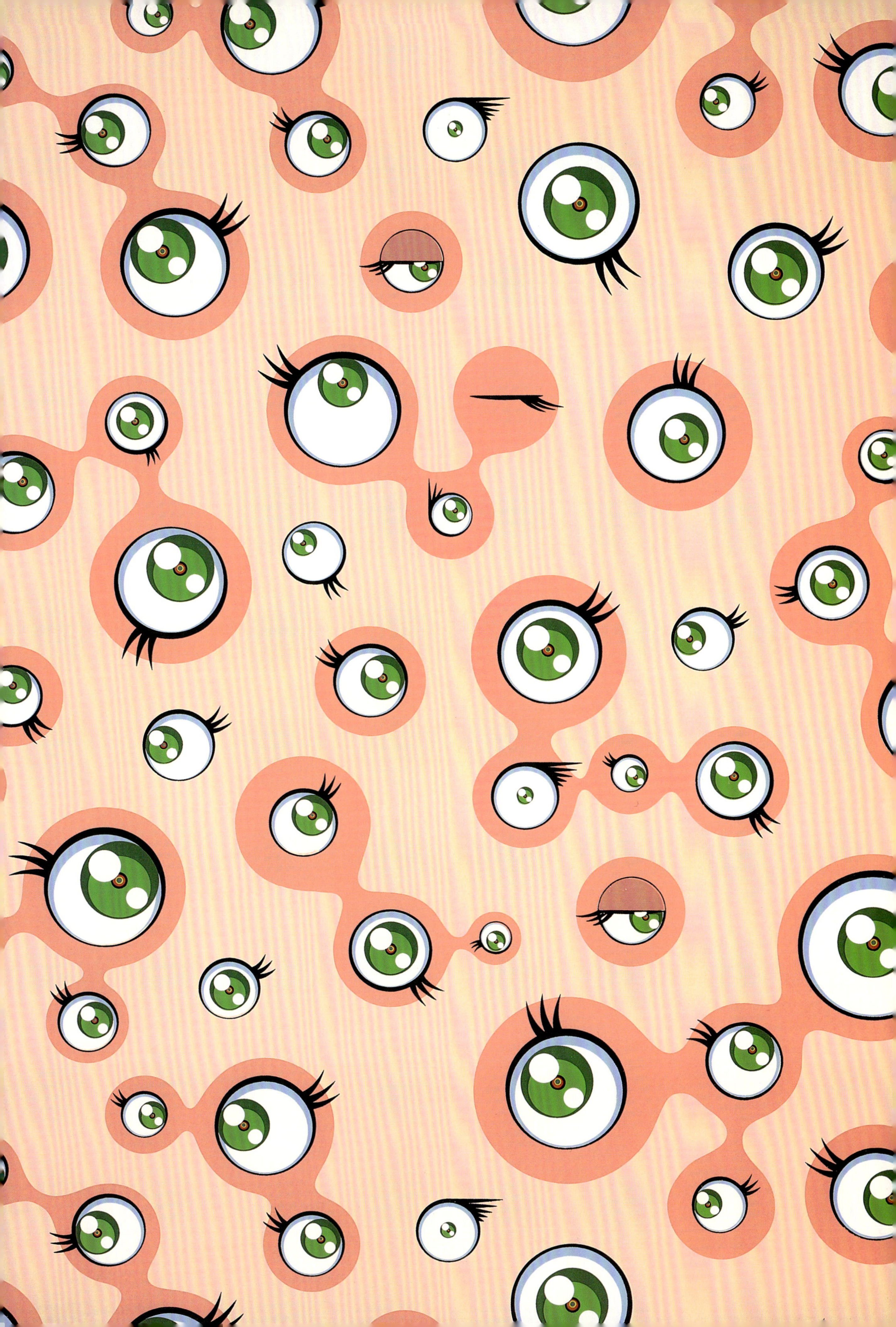

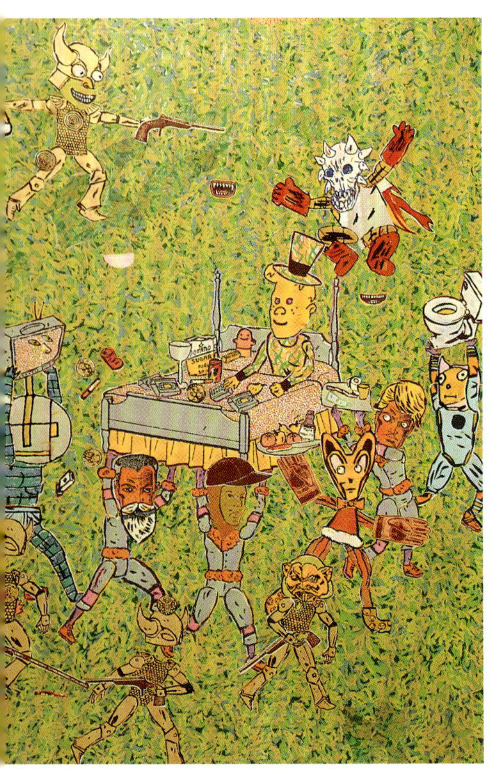

chalkboard. How perfect to convert this message years later to wallpaper, a medium associated with banality and repetition! Baldessari used wallpaper as a primary element in his *RMS W VU: Wallpaper, Lamps, and Plants. (New)*, a large installation with a shorthand title.[8] In each of four simple patterns, a pair of mundane but richly associative objects – a piece of popcorn and a nose, a pizza pie and a clock, a potato and a light bulb, a pretzel and an ear – are incongruously juxtaposed on a vividly colored ground. The individual images are commonplace, but the combinations are oddly unsettling (ills. cover and p. 6).

Ann Agee also deals with the mundane, but working by hand is at the core of her practice. *Jello Yellow Calico* is entirely hand painted, from the traditional calico background to the seemingly cut-out and collaged images of packaging for Tide detergent, Wise potato chips, Fluff marshmallow, Chinese and Mexican foods, and other household products, which are arranged into floral patterns. Whereas earlier wallpaper designs often imitated expensive materials such as chintz, brocade, and leather, Agee's appropriation of calico and product logos highlights her preference for what is easily accessible as well as colorful and richly patterned. A group of Agee's porcelain figurines of contemporary men and women was shown in The RISD Museum's Porcelain Gallery concurrently with *On the Wall*. Dressed in fabulous stripes, plaids, and polka dots and engaged in everything from taking photographs to giving birth, they are another example of the artist's interest in updating seemingly outmoded genres associated with the decorative arts.

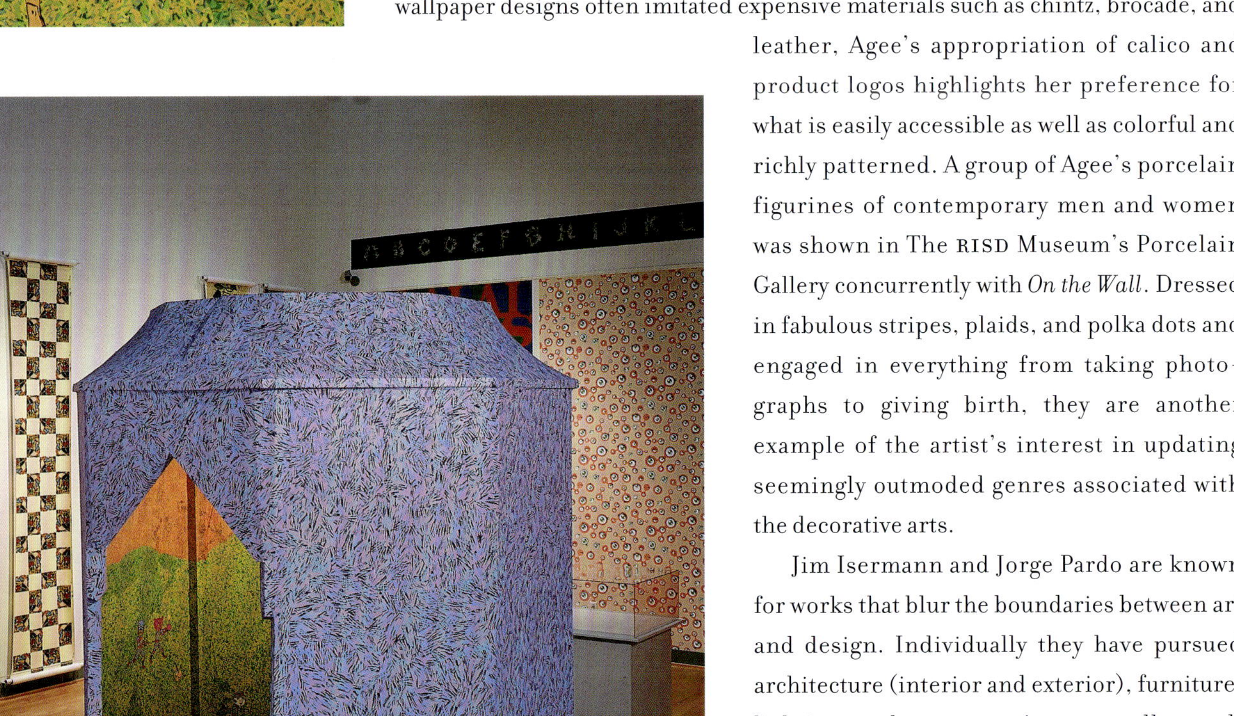

Jim Isermann and Jorge Pardo are known for works that blur the boundaries between art and design. Individually they have pursued architecture (interior and exterior), furniture, lighting, and carpet projects as well as wall coverings. Whereas the precursors of Pardo's project seem to be the more organic mid twentieth-century designs of Charles and Ray Eames and George Nelson, Isermann is rooted in geometric modular structure passed down from the Bauhaus to minimalism to 1970s supergraphics. Pardo's untitled wallpaper was created for a semipermanent space that functions as a video lounge and reception area (ill. p. 53) at The Fabric Workshop and Museum, Philadelphia. It features a loosely defined "plaid" of flowing bands of pastel color punctuated by seemingly random gestural black lines. Isermann's wall installation reconfigures silver mylar squares from a project he designed for the Portikus exhibition space in Frankfurt, Germany, in 2000. Adhering to a systematic progression, a pattern of cut-out ellipses was seen to proceed across the wall, moving from the solid silver Mylar sheets on the left to full circles revealing the underlying white wall on the right.

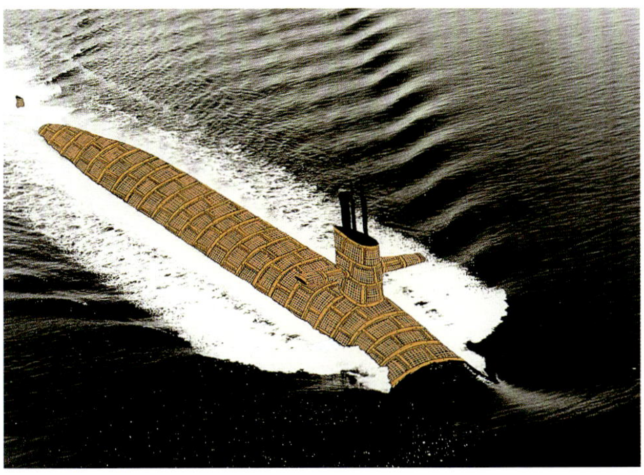

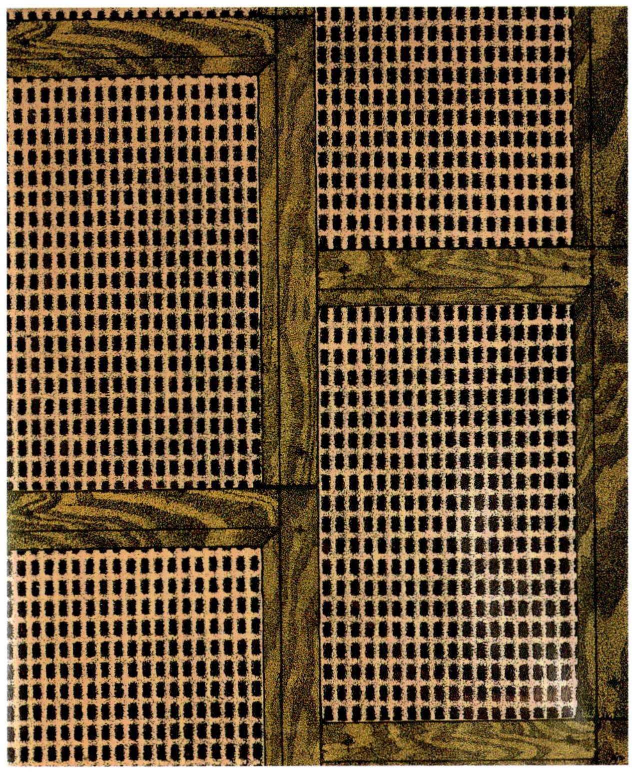

Brian Chippendale studied printmaking and has become well known as the drummer in a music duo called Lightning Bolt. For RISD's *On the Wall*, he constructed a three-dimensional modular hut entitled *The Only House I Can Afford in Providence*. The hut could be entered and featured paper walls inside and out. Chippendale built up rich webs of color by hand-screenprinting several layers of ink onto newsprint and then tore the sheets into smaller pieces and pasted them together, rather like papier-mâché. To the interior of the hut, he added collaged figural elements to create a narrative depicting war between "haves" (the landlord, for one) and "have-nots." Christine Tarkowski also explores the potential of wallpaper for architectural exteriors and public sites as well as interior spaces. In *Exposed Stud/Nuclear Sub* from her series entitled "Architectural Targets," Tarkowski proposes to cover the USS Michigan, a ballistic nuclear submarine, with wallpaper that photographically simulates and animates the two-by-four (inch) stud-and-mesh construction of a wall. With an eye to the social, political, cultural, and economic functions of a specific location, Tarkowski has at other times created but not realized wallpaper designs for a housing project and a correctional facility, and actualized such projects for an abandoned Woolworth's store and a children's advocacy center, among other sites.

Jenny Holzer's *Inflammatory Essays* have appeared since the late 1970s on storefronts, city walls, and in museums and galleries. Disturbing phrases and sentences are the primary medium through which the artist addresses who has power and how it pervades and impacts our lives, whether overtly or subliminally. Holzer adapts the tradition and format of political posters, but by using a variety of colors and arrangements for large expanses, she merges the visual with the verbal for greater impact. In his *Male and Female Genital Wallpaper*, Robert Gober interweaves simply

ABOVE: Christine Tarkowski at RISD, *Exposed Stud/Nuclear Sub*, from the "Architectural Targets" series, 1998, image: gouache on ink-jet print on paper; wallpaper: hand screenprint on paper. Courtesy of the artist

FACING PAGE, TOP: Brian Chippendale at RISD, *The Only House I Can Afford in Providence* (interior detail), 2003, hand screenprint on newspaper on wood with collaged hand-screen-printed cutouts. Courtesy of the artist

FACING PAGE, BOTTOM: Brian Chippendale (foreground), Ann Agee, Rodney Graham, William Wegman (above), Takashi Murakami (l. to r.) at RISD

YOU GET SO YOU DON'T EVEN NOTICE THE HALF-DEAD VAGRANTS ON THE STREET. THEY'RE ONLY DIRTY GHOSTS. THE ONES WHO SEND SHIVERS DOWN YOUR SPINE ARE THE UNEMPLOYED WHO AREN'T WEAK YET. THEY STILL CAN FIGHT AND RUN WHEN THEY WANT TO. THEY STILL THINK, AND THEY KNOW THEY HATE YOU. YOU WON'T BE A PRETTY SIGHT IF THEY GO FOR YOU. WHEN YOU'RE OUT WALKING, YOU LOOK AT THE MEN FOR SIGNS OF LINGERING HEALTH AND OBVIOUS HATRED. YOU EVEN WATCH THE FALLEN ONES WHO MIGHT MAKE A LAST MOVE, WHO MIGHT CLAW YOUR ANKLE AND TAKE YOU DOWN.

SENTIMENTALITY DELAYS THE REMOVAL OF THE POLITICALLY BACKWARD AND THE ORGANICALLY UNSOUND. RIGOROUS SELECTION IS MANDATORY IN SOCIAL AND GENETIC ENGINEERING. INCORRECT MERCIFUL IMPULSES POSTPONE THE CLEANSING THAT PRECEDES REFORM. SHORT-TERM NICETIES MUST YIELD TO LONG-RANGE NECESSITY. MORALS WILL BE REVISED TO MEET THE REQUIREMENTS OF TODAY. MEANINGLESS PLATITUDES WILL BE PULLED FROM TONGUES AND MINDS. WORDS LIKE "PURGE" AND "EUTHANASIA" DESERVE NEW CONNOTATIONS. THEY SHOULD BE RECOGNIZED AS THE RATIONAL PUBLIC POLICIES THEY ARE. THE GREATEST DANGER IS NOT EXCESSIVE ZEAL BUT UNDUE HESITATION. WE WILL LEARN TO IMITATE NATURE. HER KILLS NOURISH STRONG LIFE. SQUEAMISHNESS IS THE CRIME.

REPRESSING SEX URGES IS SO BAD. POISON DAMS UP INSIDE AND THEN IT MUST COME OUT. WHEN SEX IS HELD BACK TOO LONG IT COMES OUT FAST AND WILD. IT CAN DO A LOT OF HARM. INNOCENT PEOPLE GET SHOT OR CUT BY CONFUSED SEX URGES. THEY DON'T KNOW WHAT HIT THEM UNTIL TOO LATE. PARENTS SHOULD LET CHILDREN EXPRESS THEMSELVES SO THEY DON'T GET MEAN EARLY. ADULTS SHOULD MAKE SURE THEY FIND MANY OUTLETS. ALL PEOPLE SHOULD RESPOND TO BIG SEX URGES. DON'T MAKE FUN OF INDIVIDUALS AND SEND THEM AWAY. IT'S BETTER TO VOLUNTEER THAN TO GET FORCED.

DON'T TALK DOWN TO ME. DON'T BE POLITE TO ME. DON'T TRY TO MAKE ME FEEL NICE. DON'T RELAX. I'LL CUT THE SMILE OFF YOUR FACE. YOU THINK I DON'T KNOW WHAT'S GOING ON. YOU THINK I'M AFRAID TO REACT. THE JOKE'S ON YOU. I'M BIDING MY TIME, LOOKING FOR THE SPOT. YOU THINK NO ONE CAN REACH YOU, NO ONE CAN HAVE WHAT YOU HAVE. I'VE BEEN PLANNING WHILE YOU'RE PLAYING. I'VE BEEN SAVING WHILE YOU'RE SPENDING. THE GAME IS ALMOST OVER SO IT'S TIME YOU ACKNOWLEDGE ME. DO YOU WANT TO FALL NOT EVER KNOWING WHO TOOK YOU?

REPRESSING SEX URGES IS SO BAD. POISON DAMS UP INSIDE AND THEN IT MUST COME OUT. WHEN SEX IS HELD BACK TOO LONG IT COMES OUT FAST AND WILD. IT CAN DO A LOT OF HARM. INNOCENT PEOPLE GET SHOT OR CUT BY CONFUSED SEX URGES. THEY DON'T KNOW WHAT HIT THEM UNTIL TOO LATE. PARENTS SHOULD LET CHILDREN EXPRESS THEMSELVES SO THEY DON'T GET MEAN EARLY. ADULTS SHOULD MAKE SURE THEY FIND MANY OUTLETS. ALL PEOPLE SHOULD RESPOND TO BIG SEX NEEDS. DON'T MAKE FUN OF INDIVIDUALS AND SEND THEM AWAY. IT'S BETTER TO VOLUNTEER THAN TO GET FORCED.

A CRUEL BUT ANCIENT LAW DEMANDS AN EYE FOR AN EYE. MURDER MUST BE ANSWERED BY EXECUTION. ONLY GOD HAS THE RIGHT TO TAKE A LIFE AND WHEN SOMEONE BREAKS THIS LAW HE WILL BE PUNISHED. JUSTICE MUST COME SWIFTLY. IT DOESN'T HELP ANYONE TO STALL. THE VICTIM'S FAMILY CRIES OUT FOR SATISFACTION, THE COMMUNITY BEGS FOR PROTECTION AND THE DEPARTED CRAVES VENGEANCE SO HE CAN REST. THE KILLER KNEW IN ADVANCE THERE WAS NO EXCUSE FOR HIS ACT, TRULY HE HAS TAKEN HIS OWN LIFE. HE, NOT SOCIETY, IS RESPONSIBLE FOR HIS FATE. HE ALONE STANDS GUILTY AND DAMNED.

IT ALL HAS TO BURN, IT'S GOING TO BLAZE. IT IS FILTHY AND CAN'T BE SAVED. A COUPLE OF GOOD THINGS WILL BURN WITH THE REST BUT IT'S O. K., EVERY PIECE IS PART OF THE UGLY WHOLE. EVERYTHING CONSPIRES TO KEEP YOU HUNGRY AND AFRAID FOR YOUR BABIES. DON'T WAIT ANY LONGER. WAITING IS WEAKNESS, WEAKNESS IS SLAVERY. BURN DOWN THE SYSTEM THAT HAS NO PLACE FOR YOU, RISE TRIUMPHANT FROM THE ASHES. FIRE PURIFIES AND RELEASES ENERGY. FIRE GIVES HEAT AND LIGHT. LET FIRE BE THE CELEBRATION OF YOUR DELIVERANCE. LET LIGHTNING STRIKE, LET THE FLAMES DEVOUR THE ENEMY!

SENTIMENTALITY DELAYS THE REMOVAL OF THE POLITICALLY BACKWARD AND THE ORGANICALLY UNSOUND. RIGOROUS SELECTION IS MANDATORY IN SOCIAL AND GENETIC ENGINEERING. INCORRECT MERCIFUL IMPULSES POSTPONE THE CLEANSING THAT PRECEDES REFORM. SHORT-TERM NICETIES MUST YIELD TO LONG-RANGE NECESSITY. MORALS WILL BE REVISED TO MEET THE REQUIREMENTS OF TODAY. MEANINGLESS PLATITUDES WILL BE PULLED FROM TONGUES AND MINDS. WORDS LIKE "PURGE" AND "EUTHANASIA" DESERVE NEW CONNOTATIONS. THEY SHOULD BE RECOGNIZED AS THE RATIONAL PUBLIC POLICIES THEY ARE. THE GREATEST DANGER IS NOT EXCESSIVE ZEAL BUT UNDUE HESITATION. WE WILL LEARN TO IMITATE NATURE. HER KILLS NOURISH STRONG LIFE. SQUEAMISHNESS IS THE CRIME.

YOU GET SO YOU DON'T EVEN NOTICE THE HALF-DEAD VAGRANTS ON THE STREET. THEY'RE ONLY DIRTY GHOSTS. THE ONES WHO SEND SHIVERS DOWN YOUR SPINE ARE THE UNEMPLOYED WHO AREN'T WEAK YET. THEY STILL CAN FIGHT AND RUN WHEN THEY WANT TO. THEY STILL THINK, AND THEY KNOW THEY HATE YOU. YOU WON'T BE A PRETTY SIGHT IF THEY GO FOR YOU. WHEN YOU'RE OUT WALKING, YOU LOOK AT THE MEN FOR SIGNS OF LINGERING HEALTH AND OBVIOUS HATRED. YOU EVEN WATCH THE FALLEN ONES WHO MIGHT MAKE A LAST MOVE, WHO MIGHT CLAW YOUR ANKLE AND TAKE YOU DOWN.

DESTROY SUPERABUNDANCE. STARVE THE FLESH, SHAVE THE HAIR, EXPOSE THE BONE, CLARIFY THE MIND, DEFINE THE WILL, RESTRAIN THE SENSES, LEAVE THE FAMILY, FLEE THE CHURCH, KILL THE VERMIN, VOMIT THE HEART, FORGET THE DEAD. LIMIT TIME, FORGO AMUSEMENT, DENY NATURE, REJECT ACQUAINTANCES, DISCARD OBJECTS, FORGET TRUTHS, DISSECT MYTH, STOP MOTION, BLOCK IMPULSE, CHOKE SOBS, SWALLOW CHATTER. SCORN JOY, SCORN TOUCH, SCORN TRAGEDY, SCORN LIBERTY, SCORN CONSTANCY, SCORN HOPE, SCORN EXALTATION, SCORN REPRODUCTION, SCORN VARIETY, SCORN EMBELLISHMENT, SCORN RELEASE, SCORN REST, SCORN SWEETNESS, SCORN LIGHT. IT'S A QUESTION OF FORM AS MUCH AS FUNCTION. IT IS A MATTER OF REVULSION.

DON'T TALK DOWN TO ME. DON'T BE POLITE TO ME. DON'T TRY TO MAKE ME FEEL NICE. DON'T RELAX. I'LL CUT THE SMILE OFF YOUR FACE. YOU THINK I DON'T KNOW WHAT'S GOING ON. YOU THINK I'M AFRAID TO REACT. THE JOKE'S ON YOU. I'M BIDING MY TIME, LOOKING FOR THE SPOT. YOU THINK NO ONE CAN REACH YOU, NO ONE CAN HAVE WHAT YOU HAVE. I'VE BEEN PLANNING WHILE YOU'RE PLAYING. I'VE BEEN SAVING WHILE YOU'RE SPENDING. THE GAME IS ALMOST OVER SO IT'S TIME YOU ACKNOWLEDGE ME. DO YOU WANT TO FALL NOT EVER KNOWING WHO TOOK YOU?

IT'S MOSTLY LOVE THAT MAKES YOU LOOK AT FINE ANKLES AND THEN BREAK THEM. THE ANKLE IS WHERE THE MOVING POWER OF THE LEG TAPERS TO AN EXQUISITE STEM OF BONE. SADLY, THE FOOT COMES NEXT, ANCHORING WONDERFU CREATURES TO THE DIRT. DEER, WADING BIRDS AND THE BEST PEOPLE HAVE FINE ANKLES. IT'S GOOD TO CRACK THEIR SUPPORTS SO THEY'LL FALL DOWN IN AS LOVELY CURL. THEN YOU'LL CARE FOR THEM SO THEY WILL BE FREE FROM ALL CRASSNESS AND STRUGGLE. YOU'LL WATCH THE SHATTERED ANKLES HEAL AND MEANWHILE, THE CREATURES LIVE IN A STATE OF GRACE AND SUSPENDED ANIMATION.

REPRESSING SEX URGES IS SO

IT'S MOSTLY LOVE THAT MAKES

A CRUEL BUT ANCIENT LAW

drawn images of the male organ, an androgynous female torso, and other partial figures. In this provocative pattern, Gober underscores how attitudes about sexual identity "become ingrained by a process of repetition and reiteration so insidious and familiar that we neither notice nor question them."[9] Wallpaper is also aptly suited to the artist's long-standing interest in domestic objects and the home as sources for childhood memories and formative experiences.

Joan Nelson, who is known for landscape paintings that draw freely on the work of earlier artists from Renaissance masters to nineteenth-century American luminists, is represented by the lush pattern of a pumpkin vine that somewhat eerily snakes its way through an array of variously shaped leaves. In contrast to her paintings, which are usually quite small, the repeat in this wallpaper is five feet long and requires twenty-eight screens to produce. Tropical as well as temperate, the plant forms are based directly on observation but are woven together by the artist in ways that would not occur in nature. Jane Masters luxuriates in the decorative possibilities of symmetrical abstract pattern, creating a new version (in red and pink) of *Groovy*, a dynamic modular repeat that suggests an enlargement of embroidery or lace (ill. p. 5). At the same time that she pays tribute to pre-industrial craftspersons for their dexterity and commitment, Masters playfully pays homage to Bridget Riley (British, b. 1931) and Victor Vasarely (French, b. Hungary, 1908–97) for their obsessively controlled but simultaneously vibrant Op art paintings.

Virgil Marti's dazzling *Lotus Room* installation features a checkerboard of salmon-pink lotus blossoms screenprinted on silver mylar and interspersed with collaged bonsai driftwood elements that sprout the occasional ranunculus, hydrangea, or spider chrysanthemum. Marti's inspiration runs from the textile patterns of Japanese Nō theater robes and the *chinoiseries* of the Brighton Pavilion to the kitsch and pop culture of his childhood and adolescence in the 1960s and 70s. Whereas Marti's earlier wallpaper projects explored issues of identity through taste, class distinctions, and the psychology of decorating, he now seamlessly interweaves his current interests in architecture and the history of decorative arts into the mix (ill. p. 2).

In Matthew Benedict's painting *The House of the Seven Gables*, based on the classic Nathaniel Hawthorne novel (1851), wallpaper provides subject matter as

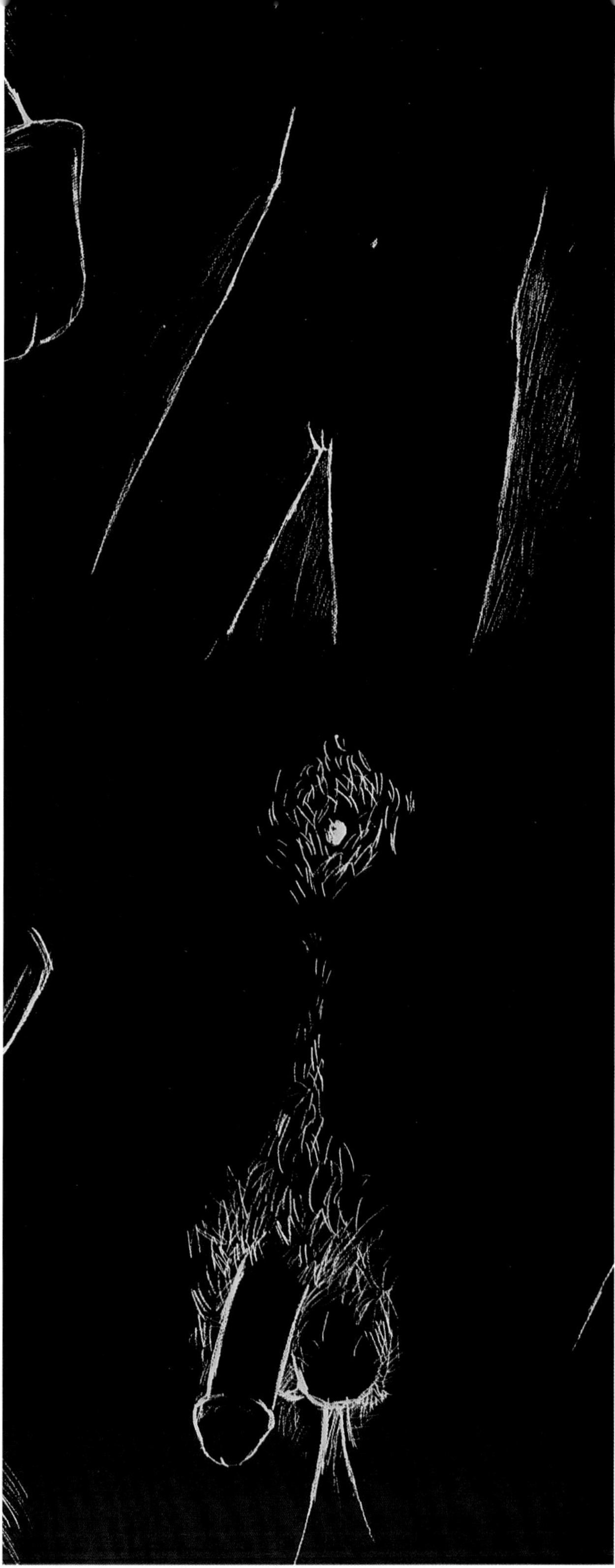

ABOVE: Robert Gober at RISD, *Male and Female Genital Wallpaper*, 1989, hand screenprint on paper. Courtesy of the artist

FACING PAGE: Jenny Holzer, *Inflammatory Essays*, 1979–82, offset print on paper. Courtesy of the artist and Cheim & Read, New York

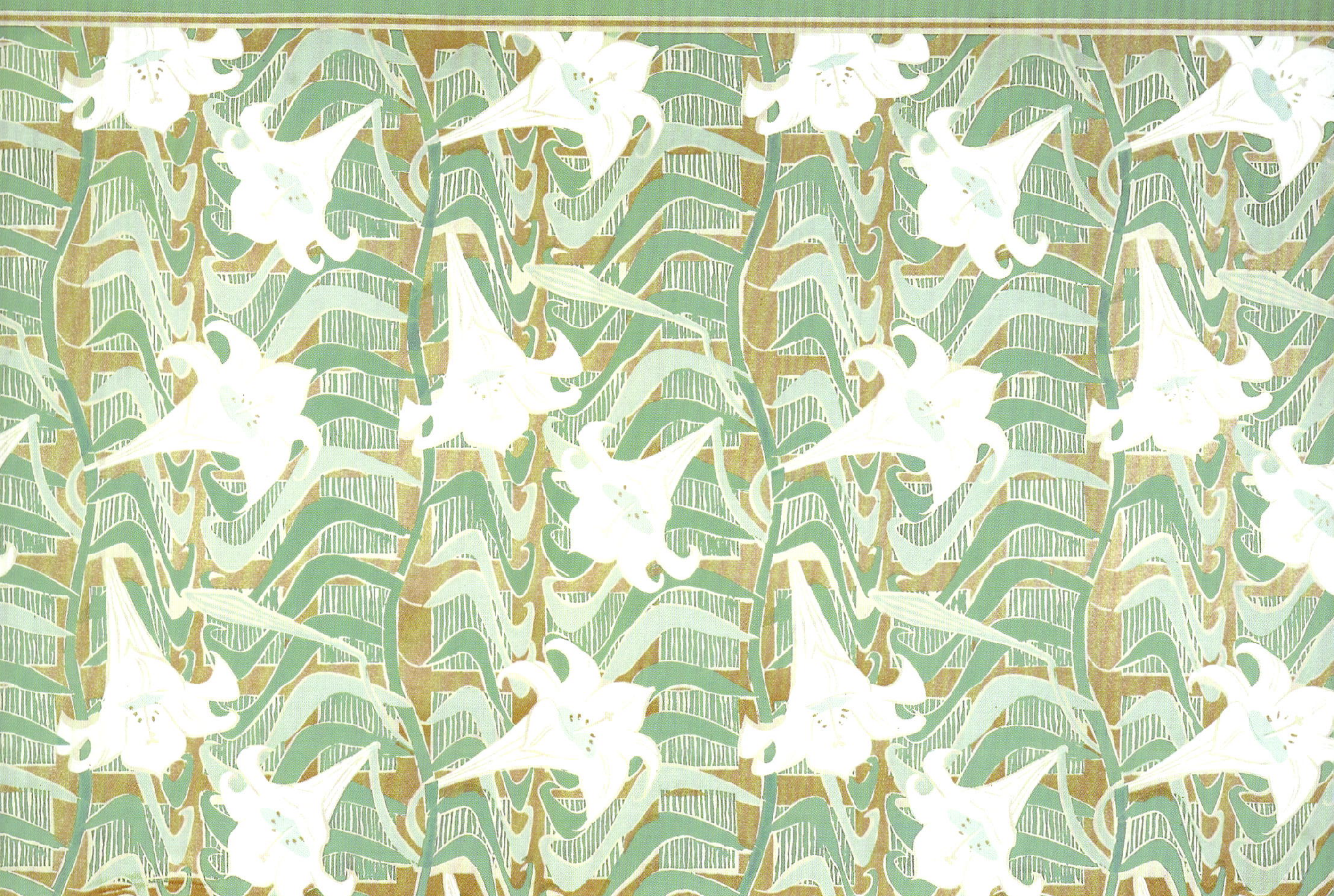

Virgil Marti, *For Oscar Wilde*, 1995, hand screen-print on paper-backed cotton sateen. Printed with the assistance of The Fabric Workshop and Museum. Collection of Marion Boulton Stroud

well as style. Depicted in gouache with the flatness and palette of a Zuber scenic paper, a central inset of the gabled house is surrounded by a garland of images that refer directly to the author, characters, and events in the book. The icing on seven gingerbread cookies spells out the curse perpetuated within the dwelling: "God will give him blood to drink." A partial white doorway on the right side of the panel places the viewer in the interior of this macabre wallpapered room.

If Oscar Wilde were on his deathbed today instead of a century ago, perhaps he would have to revise his often cited words: "My wallpaper is killing me, one of us must go." Wallpaper, as currently designed and referred to by contemporary artists, is no longer limited to decorative coverings for the walls of dining room, bedroom, or kitchen. Wallpaper may maintain its decorative function, which is not insignificant or irrelevant, but it may also do much more than that. Artists are extending the styles, techniques, and traditions of wall coverings in works that have personal meaning and at the same time define larger public issues.

1 The author has referred to Marilyn Oliver Hapgood's *Wallpaper and the Artist: From Dürer to Warhol* (New York: 1992) and expresses her debt to this valuable resource.

2 Founders' statement of purpose, March 22, 1877, set forth initially in the By-Laws of Rhode Island School of Design; see Elsie S. Bronson, *The Rhode Island School of Design: A Half-Century Record (1878–1928)*. Providence: 1928, n.p. (typewritten copies in the RISD Library). This mission statement is still in effect. It reads in full:

1. The instruction of artisans in drawing, painting, modeling and designing so that they may successfully apply the principles of art to the requirements of trade and manufacture.

2. The systematic training of students in the practice of art in order that they may understand its principles, give instruction to others and become artists.

3. The general advancement of public art education by the collection and exhibition of works of art and by lectures and by other means of instruction in the fine arts.

3 Old Westbury, New York: 1973; first published 1893; reprinted by Small, Maynard, Boston, 1899.

4 Two panels of this suite were on view in The RISD Museum's Works on Paper Gallery (*Historic Wallpapers: 1750–1949*, January 17–April 6, 2003) during the run of *On the Wall* in Providence.

5 See *Apocalyptic Wallpaper: Robert Gober, Abigail Lane, Virgil Marti, and Andy Warhol*. Columbus: 1997, p. 34.

6 See *Carrie Mae Weems*. Philadelphia: 1994, p. 13. The endpapers and illustrations of Shaw's book were designed by wood engraver John Farleigh (British, 1900–65). When first published, both text and artwork caused a sensation.

7 Conversation with the artist, June 2002.

8 Exhibited at the Museum für Gegenwartskunst Zürich and Witte de With, Rotterdam, 1998.

9 *Apocalyptic Wallpaper: Robert Gober, Abigail Lane, Virgil Marti, and Andy Warhol*. Columbus: 1997, p. 38.

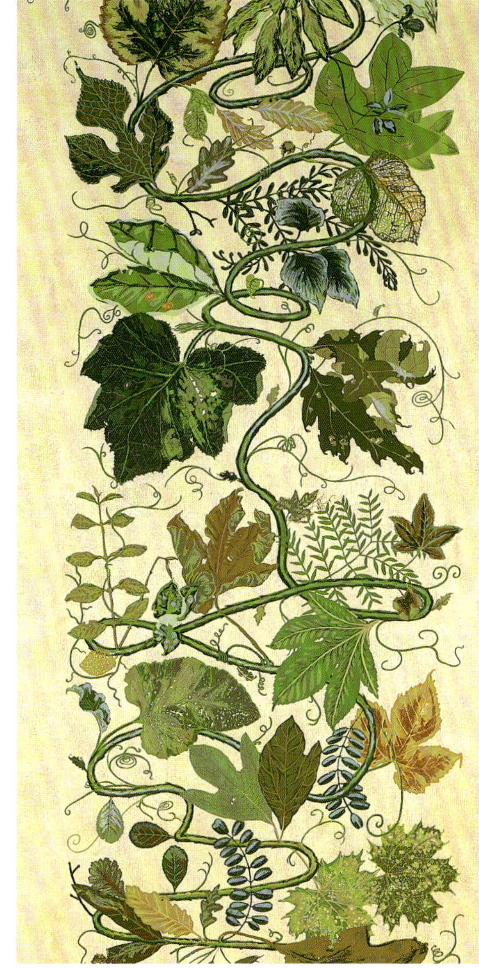

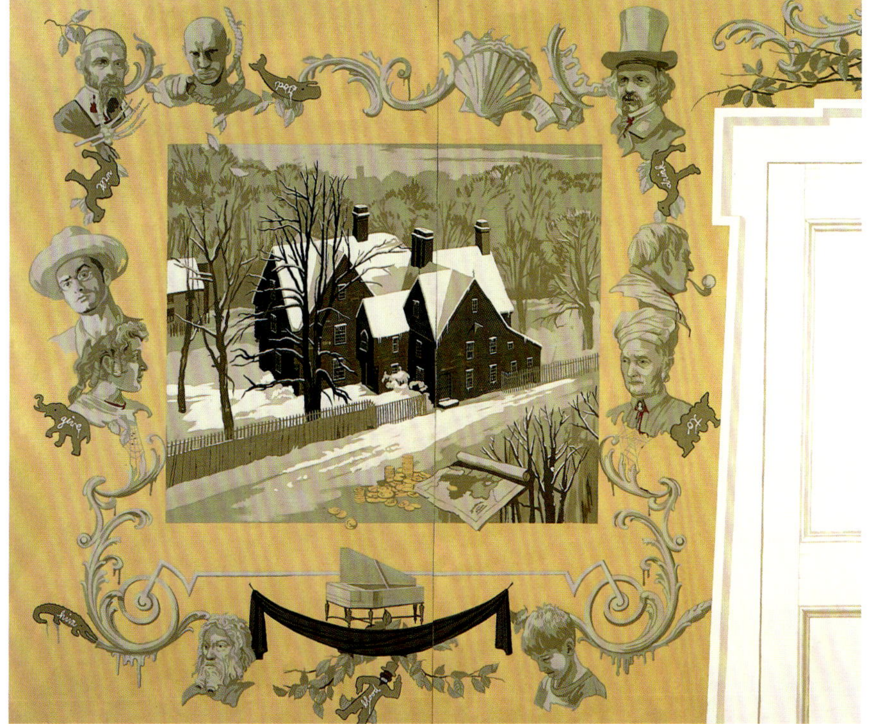

ABOVE: Joan Nelson at RISD, *Wallpaper*, 1991, hand screenprint on paper. Collection of The RISD Museum. Gift of A/D Gallery

LEFT: Matthew Benedict at RISD, *The House of the Seven Gables*, 1998, gouache on wood. Courtesy of the artist and Alexander and Bonin, New York. Image by Orcutt and Van der Putten

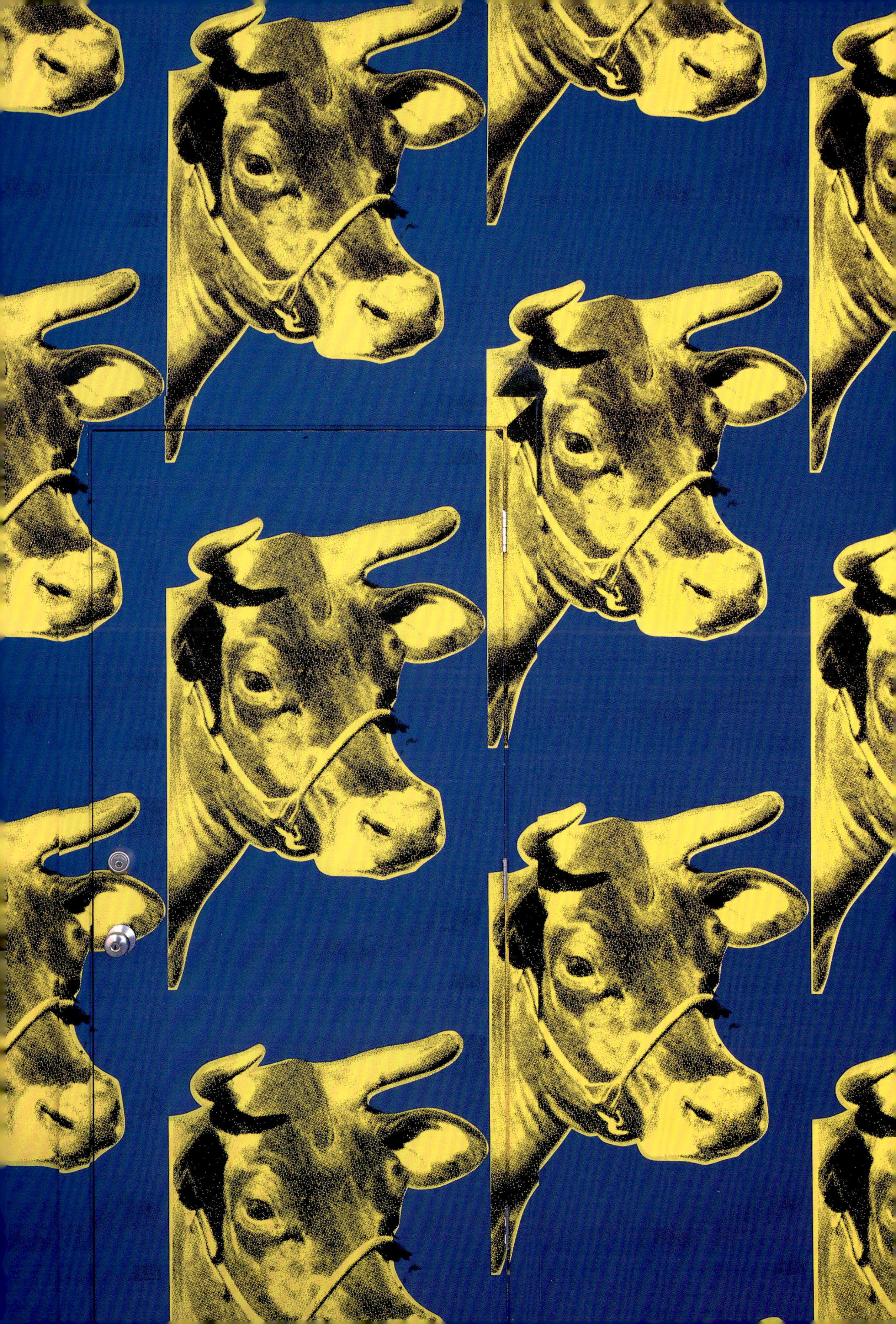

CHARLES F. STUCKEY
School of the Art Institute of Chicago

wallpaper as art *a brief history*

Works executed on walls constitute one of the most ancient and extensive categories of art, extending back some thirty thousand years to images in caves. Even so, wallpaper in art history is seldom addressed.[1] It was not until around 1500 that wallpaper became feasible – as a luxury item – thanks to technological advances in paper production and printing.[2] Although the design of wallpapers has always been artistic, in most cases the status of wallpaper as art has mostly gone unacknowledged since paper wall covering became a common household item after the advent of the Industrial Revolution and mass-production techniques. There are very few surviving wallpapered rooms from before the twentieth century, and visual documentation for art interiors is remarkably scanty.[3]

The rapid growth of museums in the nineteenth century enhanced the status of modern art produced to be collected, but wallpaper, which is manufactured for consumption rather than for preservation, has been at a disadvantage in the museum era. Moreover, due to its sudden widespread availability at low cost around 1850, wallpaper was stigmatized as a commonplace substitute for luxury décor. Of necessity, painters of interior subjects began to include wallpaper backgrounds as a sorry fact of modern life. William Holman Hunt's *The Awakening Conscience*, 1853 (Tate Gallery of British Art, London), featured a wallpaper showing a cornfield as one among many home furnishings indicative of the moral decay associated with Victorian consumerism. Commenting upon this particular work, John Ruskin condemned such middle-class excesses for their "fatal newness." Presumably, the tawdry wallpaper behind the reclining female in Eduoard Manet's *Olympia*, 1863 (Musée d'Orsay, Paris), served specifically to evoke the vulgarity of a prostitute's love nest. Most often, however, such pioneers of modern painting as Manet and Gustave Courbet, following a seventeenth-century Old Master convention, preferred shadowy monochromatic backgrounds for their works with indoor settings.

Negative attitudes about wallpaper were effectively countered by a brilliant modern-design arts community based in London, which included Sir Henry Cole, Owen Jones, William Morris, and the artists associated with the Pre-Raphaelite

FACING PAGE: Andy Warhol at FWM, *Cow Wallpaper* (blue/yellow colorway), 1966; refabricated for the Andy Warhol Museum, Pittsburgh, 1994; hand screenprint on paper. Courtesy of the Andy Warhol Museum, Pittsburgh. © 2003 Andy Warhol Foundation for the Visual Arts/ARS, New York

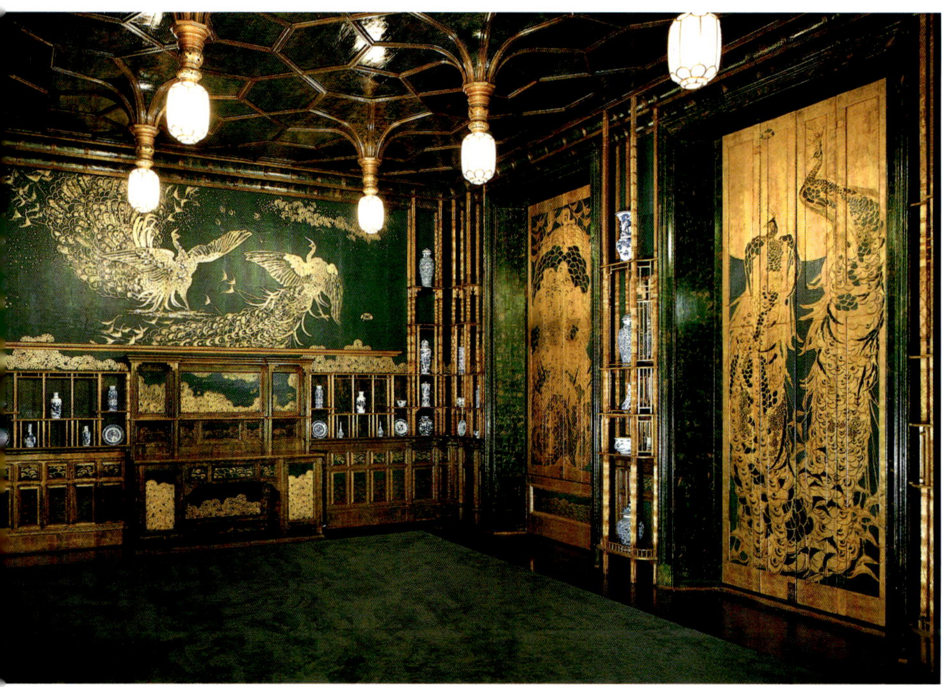

James Abbott McNeill Whistler, American, 1834–1903, *Harmony in Blue and Gold: The Peacock Room* (southeast view), 1876–77, oil paint and gold leaf on canvas, leather, and wood, 13′10″ x 32′10″ x 19′9″ (room). Freer Gallery of Art, Smithsonian Institution, Washington, DC. Gift of Charles Lang Freer, F1904. Image courtesy of Freer Gallery of Art

Brotherhood. As the name of this group suggests, the Pre-Raphaelites advocated a return to late-medieval models of surface decoration. They stressed the ancient and universal heritage of elementary patterning, predicated on the capacity of line and color in the abstract to affect mood. Stimulated by the great international exhibitions of the 1850s and 1860s, the veneration of rhythmic patterns and flat unshaded planes of color revolutionized the fundamental terms of modern painting in Great Britain. After the Great Exhibition of 1851 in London's Hyde Park with its unveiling of the Crystal Palace, Cole spearheaded efforts to create a museum specifically for the decorative arts. The result was the South Kensington Museum, since 1899 known as the Victoria and Albert Museum.

This London showplace immediately inspired similar institutions in other cities. Although hardly enough to stimulate a competitive market of wallpaper collectors, these decorative arts museums began to form their own study collections of wallpaper samples. More significantly, decorative arts museums endorsed the concept that a room as a whole could deserve consideration as an ambitious work of art. With the exception of art in churches or ceremonial government spaces, there were no venues for the public exhibition of room art until the middle of the nineteenth century; but by 1866, the South Kensington Museum was commissioning rooms as decorative-art paradigms, most famously, the wallpapered Green Dining Room by Morris, Marshall, Faulkner, and Company. Such museum acknowledgment bolstered private patronage of artist-designed rooms and encouraged artists to consider an expansion of their traditional specialist roles.

In response to the Pre-Raphaelites' decorative-arts activities, expatriate American printmaker and painter James Abbott McNeill Whistler assumed responsibility for creating overall visual environments, such as his famous *Peacock Room*, 1876–77 (now in the Freer Gallery of Art, Washington, DC), commissioned by collector Frederick Leyland, an avid patron of Morris wallpapers. Morris-style wall treatments were antithetical to Whistler's conception of architectural décor, which he derived from so-called Japonism, the far-reaching enthusiasm for Japanese aesthetics after the opening of that isolated country to Westerners in

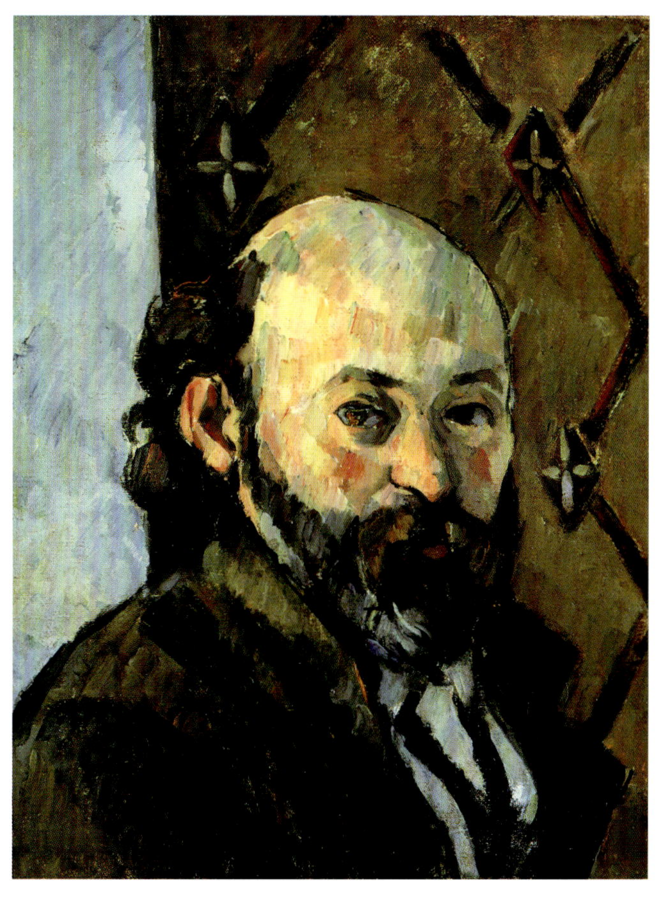

Paul Cézanne, French, 1839–1906, *Self-Portrait*, ca. 1881, oil on canvas, 13 3/32 x 10 5/32. © National Gallery, London. Image courtesy of National Gallery, London

1855. Essential to Japanese taste was the contrast between decorated and undecorated surfaces. Walls were generally blank. Nonetheless, when Whistler asserted that "the painter [ought] also make of the wall upon which his work is hung, the room containing it, the whole house, a Harmony, a Symphony, an Arrangement, as perfect as the picture or print which became a part of it,"[4] he was stating an opinion already espoused by Morris. In 1886, Whistler went so far as to wallpaper a London art gallery with plain brown wrapping paper as a chic background for an exhibition of his watercolors and pastels.

Wallpaper design soon captured the imagination of many modern-minded painters in Paris. In his *Grammaire des arts décoratifs. Décoration intérieure de la maison* (Paris: 1882), Charles Blanc devoted an entire chapter to wallpaper. Beginning in 1877, Cézanne incorporated wallpaper backgrounds into his still lifes, portraits, and self-portraits, as if to suggest that his own painter's priorities were sympathetic to flat geometric patterning. With reference to Cézanne's *Self-Portrait*, ca. 1881 (Tate Gallery of Modern Art, London), Meyer Schapiro wrote: "This wedding of the organic [figure] and the geometric has a beautiful simplicity which makes us overlook or accept the arbitrary treatment of the wallpaper pattern. The ornament is not used for surface interest, but as a necessary element of structure in a whole of great concentration and weight."[5]

Paul Gauguin owned a Cézanne still life with a wallpaper background, and in 1890, the younger artist incorporated this into one of his own paintings (now in the Art Institute of Chicago) as background to emphasize the significance of pattern for modern art. As early as 1881, Gauguin had begun including patterned wall coverings as backgrounds in his paintings in order to establish specific moods. For example, the birds represented as background décor in a child's bedroom might suggest flights of imagination. Writing to Vincent van Gogh, Gauguin explained the wallpaper represented in an 1888 self-portrait (Van Gogh Museum, Amsterdam; Vincent van Gogh Foundation): "The girlish background, with its childlike flowers is there to attest to our artistic purity."[6] Van Gogh immediately adopted the wallpaper background concept for his own rather Pre-Raphaelite portraits of members of the Roulin family.

Under the spell of van Gogh and Gauguin, the young Nabis painters made a veritable cult of decoration in the 1890s.[7] Maurice Denis exhibited wallpaper designs in Paris in 1893, including one arabesque pattern with a railroad train. In his experimental novel *Textes & Opinions du Docteur Faustroll*, 1898, French writer

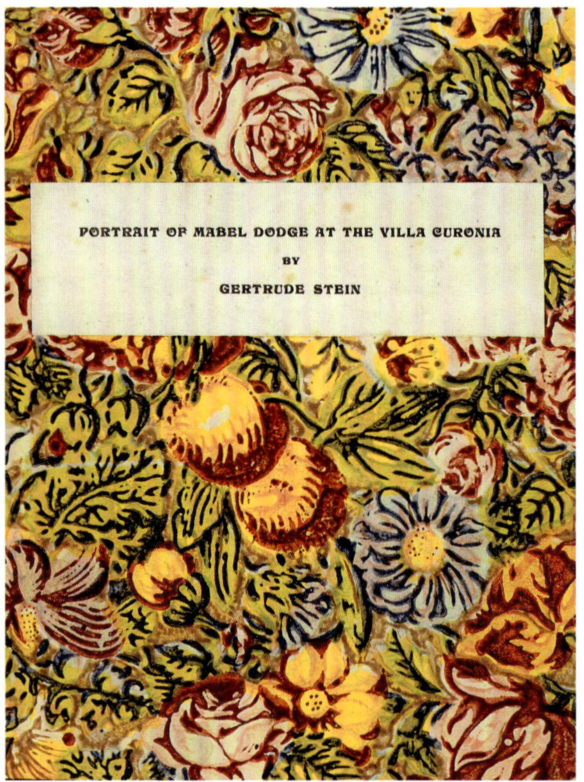

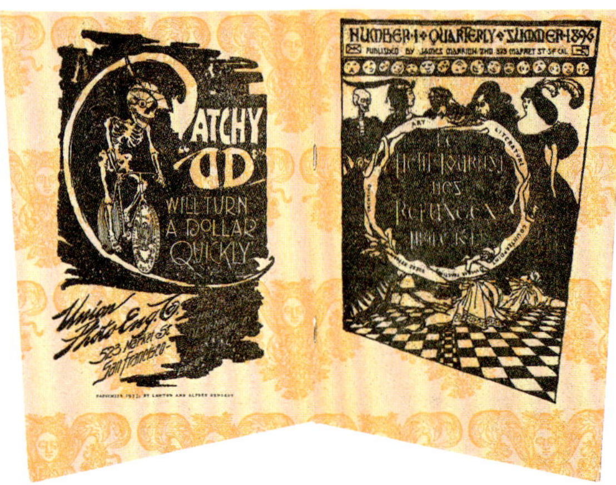

TOP: Gertrude Stein, American, 1874–1946, *Portrait of Mabel Dodge at the Villa Curonia*, 1912 (cover); privately printed for Mabel Dodge at the Galileiana Press, Florence. Courtesy of the Estate of Gertrude Stein, through its Literary Executor, Mr. Stanford Gann, Jr., of Levin & Gann, P.A. Image courtesy of Yale Collection of American Literature, Beinecke Rare Book and Manuscript Library, Yale University

ABOVE: Cover and back page of the facsimile edition of Gellett Burgess and Porter Garnett, *Le Petit Journal des Refusées*, originally published 1896, facsimile published as *California Magazines*, the 1975 Keepsake Edition by the Book Club of California. Image courtesy of the Book Club of California

Alfred Jarry, with characteristic humor, has the protagonist take a sponge bath in Denis's train wallpaper! It is possible that Jarry had in mind the sort of contemporary images created by Edouard Vuillard, which incorporate so many different fabrics and wall coverings that the figures all but drown in seas of patterns.

Paintings conceived for ensemble installation (either in terms of shape, color, or grouping) as a fundamental feature of a particular room were referred to as "*décorations*." In the opinion of his friends, Claude Monet's paintings made in series (such as the Rouen Cathedral paintings) were foremost *décorations*, ensembles to be exhibited together under ideal circumstances, even if most of them were marketed separately. It is worth mentioning that before the 1895 exhibition of the Rouen Cathedral paintings, a single collector had bought four of them. In addition to such patronage, the example of dealer Samuel Bing's highly publicized Maison de l'Art Nouveau gallery, which opened in December 1895, seemingly prompted Monet to embark upon his famous water-lilies paintings in 1898 specifically as décor for a dining room. By the late 1890s, Bing was commissioning artists such as Henry van de Velde to design model utilitarian rooms for display in his lavish Paris gallery.[8] The rooms, some with wallpaper, may not have been expected to sell as wholes, yet their public display greatly encouraged artist-decorated rooms as entities in themselves.

More and more, as at the 1900 World's Fair in Paris, designer rooms competed for attention at art exhibitions with individual paintings or sculptures, while entire period rooms began to appeal to museums and private collectors. In 1903, the Metropolitan Museum of Art, New York, acquired a room that had been excavated from an ancient villa outside Roman Pompeii; and in 1904, Charles Freer bought Whistler's *Peacock Room* in order to incorporate it into the museum he intended to build in Washington, DC. Before World War I, whole designer rooms were sometimes included in large contemporary art exhibitions.

Wallpaper permeated the Paris art world by the fall of 1912, when the controversy over experimental Cubism was at its height. Towards the end of his summer vacation, Georges Braque (who came from a family of housepainters) bought a roll of wallpaper simulating wood paneling and pasted fragments of it into his drawings. Quickly following suit, his friend Pablo Picasso incorporated wallpapers into his own *papiers collées* (collages) no later than October 1912, along with scraps of sheet music and newsprint.[9] True enough, Picasso's Cubism was grounded in the art of Cézanne with its emphasis on patterning as compositional structure; but the wallpaper collage elements in Picasso's works are no more significantly related to Cézanne's paintings with wallpaper than they are to the ongoing Pre-Raphaelite/Nabis cult of pattern so evident in many of Matisse's works beginning around 1908.

Meanwhile, at the Salon d'Automne of 1912, which opened on October 1, a group of artists associated with Raymond Duchamp-Villon presented what they called a Cubist House (La Maison cubiste) with framed drawings and paintings installed in a furnished interior with patterned wallpaper. Wallpapered interiors by female designers associated with Paul Poiret's Paris shop, Martine, were also on view in the same exhibition. All of these works seemingly relate to an extraordinary book-object (at least we might call it that today) created at this same time, when Gertrude Stein's privately printed *Portrait of Mabel Dodge at the Villa Curonia*, 1912, was bound in Florentine wallpaper. It is worth noting that Stein may have taken inspiration from her soulmate Alice B. Toklas's friend, the San Francisco humorist Gelett Burgess (1866-1951), whose early interviews with Picasso and Braque are essential to the history of Cubism. In 1896, Burgess used actual wallpaper samples on which to print the text of his satirical single-issue journal *Le Petit Journal des Refusés*. Remarkably, Burgess's 1895 poem "The Purple Cow" ("I never saw a purple cow, / I never hope to see one...") is sometimes regarded as an inspiration for Andy Warhol's *Cow Wallpaper*. As for the role of wallpaper in classic Cubism, there is no better instance than a 1914 *Still Life* (Museum Ludwig, Cologne) by the Russian artist Liubov Popova, which prominently includes the letters "WALLPA." Popova came to Paris to study modern art in November 1912.

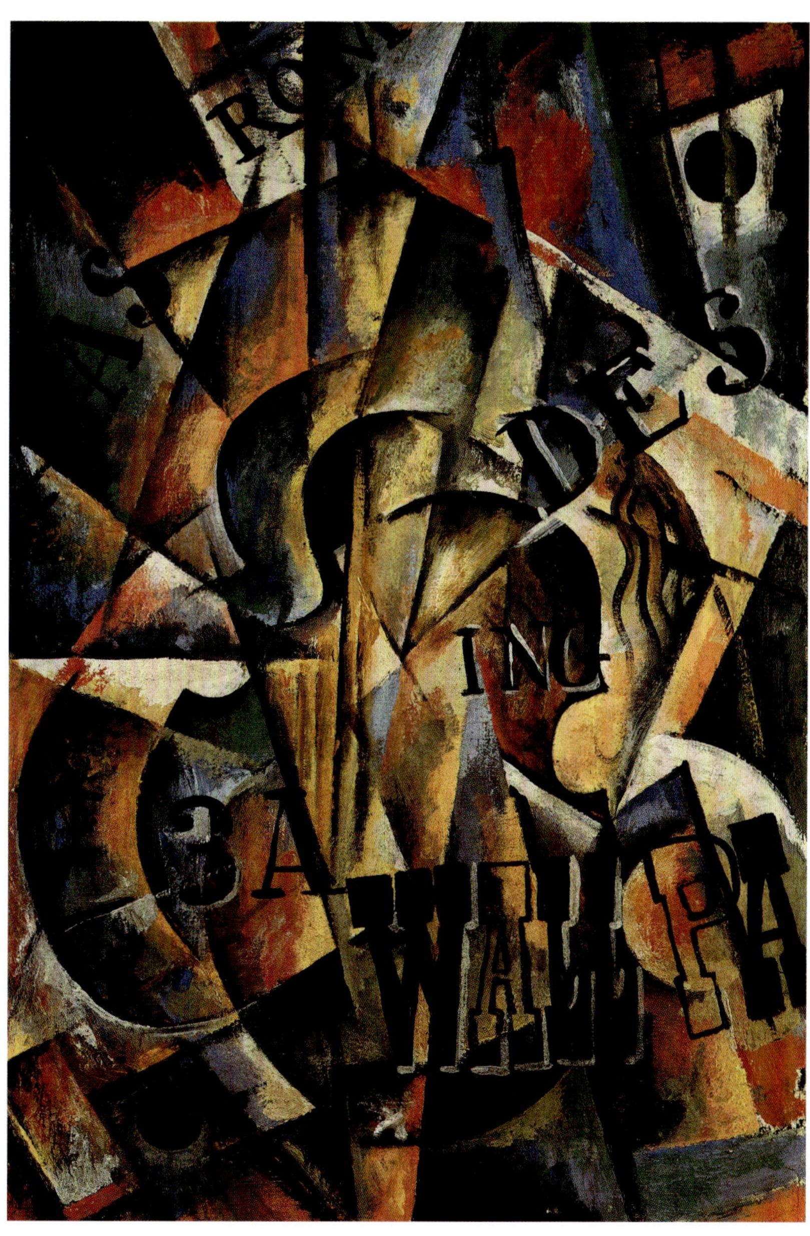

Liubov Popova, Russian, 1889-1924, *Still Life*, 1914, oil on canvas, 34 5/8 x 22 5/8. Courtesy of Museum Ludwig, Cologne. Image courtesy of Rheinisches Bildarchiv, Cologne

Despite the advocacy of Picasso and Matisse regarding surface pattern, after World War I the very idea of wallpaper became antithetical to modernist style, based primarily on the spare Arts and Crafts attitude of Frank Lloyd Wright and its heritage in the ascetic interiors of the de Stijl movement, the Bauhaus, and

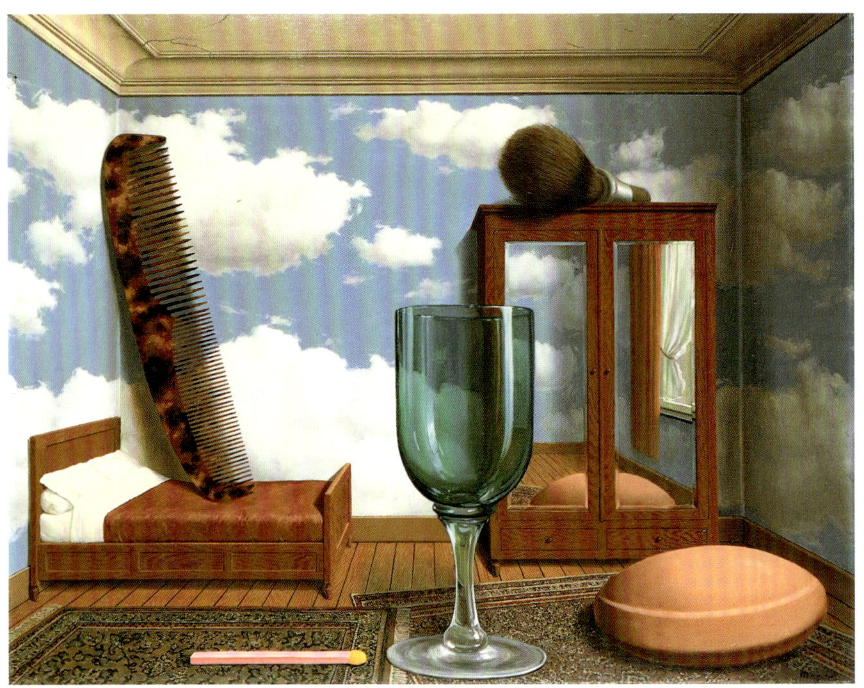

René Magritte, Belgian, 1898–1967, *Personal Values*, 1952, oil on canvas, 31 1/2 x 39 3/8. Collection of the San Francisco Museum of Modern Art, Purchased through a gift of Phyllis Wattis. Image © SFMOMA. Image by Ben Blackwell

International Style designers and architects. Increasingly, the thoughtful up-to-date display of paintings and sculpture became predicated on neutral white walls with as little ornamentation as possible.

Some notable painters designed wallpapers for commercial manufacture during the Art Deco years; among them, Raoul Dufy, Charles Burchfield, René Magritte, and even Joseph Cornell. Still, they tended to keep their careers as painters separate from their decorative-art projects. After Cubism, references to wallpaper in paintings tended to be satirical, aimed at the old-fashioned vulgarity of middle-class taste. Marcel Duchamp's assisted "ready-made," *Apolinère Enameled*, 1916–17 (Philadelphia Museum of Art), shows a wallpapered interior with a girl in the process of making her own "readymade," transforming a dated bedstead by painting it. In the 1930s, when Duchamp acted as interior decorator for his companion Mary Reynolds, he pasted maps all over a wall of her Paris apartment instead of using ordinary wallpaper. As if to appeal to any and every taste in interiors, Francis Picabia in 1919 transformed an empty frame into an assemblage, the *Danse de Saint Guy* (Centre Georges Pompidou, Paris) by stretching a few strings across it. Visible as a result of the object's openness, any wall on which this artwork is displayed becomes incorporated into it, just as the surrounding or underlying décor inevitably appears in works by Picabia's friends, whether observed through the transparent surfaces of Duchamp's works in glass or the reflective surfaces of Brancusi's polished bronzes.

Coincidentally, the integration of art and room in these highly unconventional works paralleled the heyday for the acquisition of period rooms by museums in the 1920s, ranging historically from ancient times to the present. In the opinion of Museum of Modern Art director Alfred Barr, "probably the most famous single room of twentieth-century art in the world" was El Lissitsky's 1927–28 *Abstract Cabinet*, commissioned by the Landesmuseum in Hannover. Lázsló Moholy-Nagy would also create a room for the same art museum in 1930.[10] The Musée Claude Monet, opened at the Orangerie in Paris in 1927, consisted of two oval rooms designed specifically for the artist's *Nymphéas (Water Lilies)* murals, which were glued to the walls to make removal impossible. Not intended for any function or ceremony whatsoever, these are probably the first public spaces ever established exclusively for art reverie.

Such spaces have proliferated since the end of World War II. In response to the exhibition of assertive and demanding eighteen-foot-wide paintings by Jackson Pollock, Barnett Newman, and Clyfford Still at the Betty Parsons Gallery, New York, around 1950, an enthusiasm developed for wall-to-wall, floor-to-ceiling, and even wrap-around-the-room artworks, all with inevitable wallpaper overtones. Famously, critic Harold Rosenberg in 1952 referred to large Abstract Expressionist paintings as "apocalyptic wallpaper."[11]

Around that time, it was René Magritte who most specifically addressed the wallpaper-as-art concept. He had included patterned wallpapers as bourgeois background in *The Pebble*, 1948 (Musées Royaux des Beaux-Arts de Belgique, Brussels), and *The Survivor*, 1950 (The Menil Collection, Houston); and in 1953, he completed his most ambitious mural decoration for the Casino in Knokke-le-Zoute, the eight panels of which have backgrounds of clouds, curtains, or wallpaper patterning. Themes of interior decoration took on special significance

Mike Bidlo at FWM, *R. Mutt Wallpaper*, 1997/2002, offset print on newsprint. Printed with the assistance of The Fabric Workshop and Museum. Courtesy of the artist and Galerie Bruno Bischofberger, Zürich

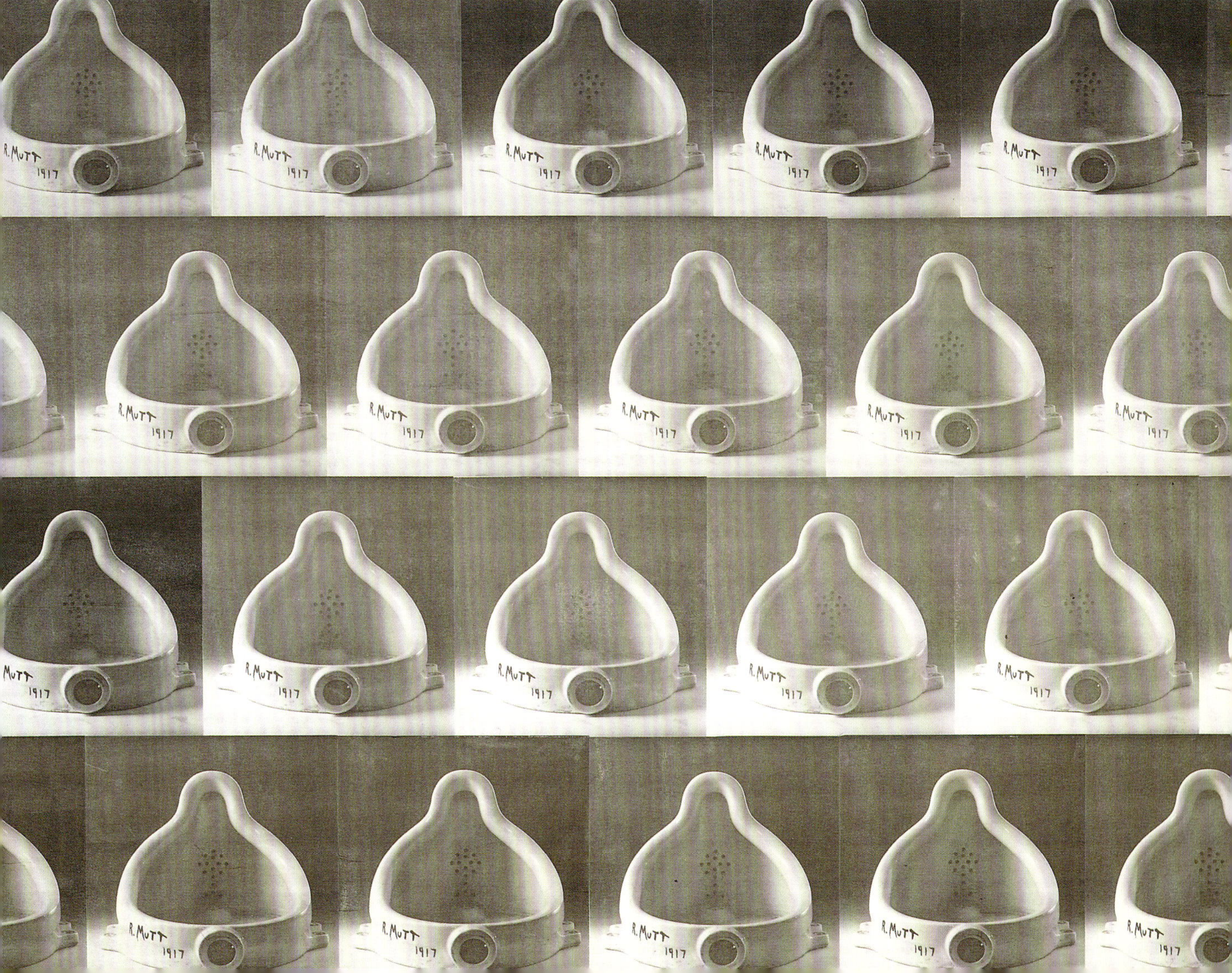

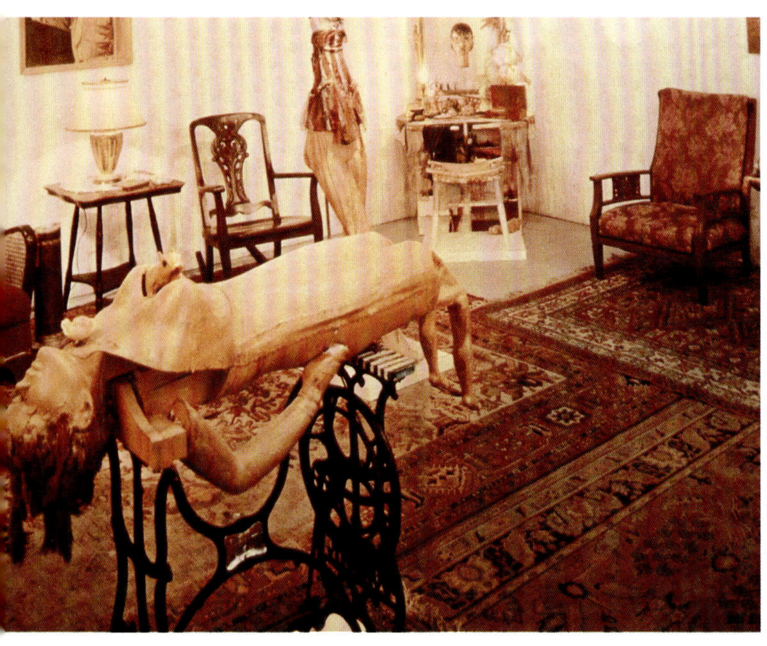

Edward Kienholz, American, 1927-94, *Roxy's*, 1961, room installation, mixed media assemblage. Collection Reinhold Onnasch, Berlin. © Nancy Reddin Kienholz. Image courtesy of L.A. Louver, Venice, California

in his conventional easel paintings around this time. In several, he repeated unit images (a man in a bowler hat or a loaf of French bread, for example) wallpaper-wise at equal intervals, thus demonstrating the sublimity of repetition and pattern in surreal fashion. Other paintings showed strange interior walls made of living rock or sky. The room depicted in *Personal Values*, 1952 (Museum of Modern Art, San Francisco), has walls decorated with clouds on blue, as if they were made of glass, revealing the outside sky surrounding some isolated skyscraper's heavenly upper floor.

During the 1950s, several artists who had nothing the least to do with wallpaper nevertheless stressed the walls of the display room in an unprecedented way, thus initiating what is today called installation art. In the late 1950s and 60s, such work was more often referred to as an "environment," and with some justification, Louise Nevelson credited herself with inventing the genre. Given the scale and complexity of her wall-hugging pieces, however, they seldom appear in museum surveys highlighting that time period. In this context, it would be wrong not to mention Yves Klein's *Le Vide*, presented at the Galerie Iris Clert, Paris, in 1958. Having painted over the gallery windows with his hallmark blue, Klein otherwise left the walls bare – an empty room filled with priceless nothing to sell or to possess.

Wallpaper itself did play a part in work by some of the artists who pursued the creation of "environments" and room art in the late 1950s and early 60s. Edward Kienholz's *Roxy's* (Collection Reinhold Onnasch, Berlin) was exhibited at the Alexander Iolas Gallery, New York, in 1963. Kienholz included walls separate from those of the gallery in this life-size evocation of a Nevada whorehouse, complete with tacky wallpaper. Around 1964, James Rosenquist used patterned paint rollers to imprint several of his complex Pop masterpieces with wallpaper patterns, including *Lanai*, 1964 (ex-collection John and Kimiko Powers).

As if in response to recent works by Kienholz, Rosenquist, and others, as well as to the Museum of Modern Art's 1960 exhibition of Monet's works in series, Andy Warhol brought wallpaper into its own in 1966 with an April exhibition at the Leo Castelli Gallery, New York. Warhol presented a room hung all around with his *Cow Wallpaper*. The space contained nothing else, effectively extending Klein's idea of a commercial exhibition with no art for sale. Although they were little more than relics of Warhol's masterpiece environment, clients could purchase rolls of the printed paper, just as they might collect an unframed print for display. Warhol signed somewhere around a hundred to a hundred and fifty wallpaper samples.

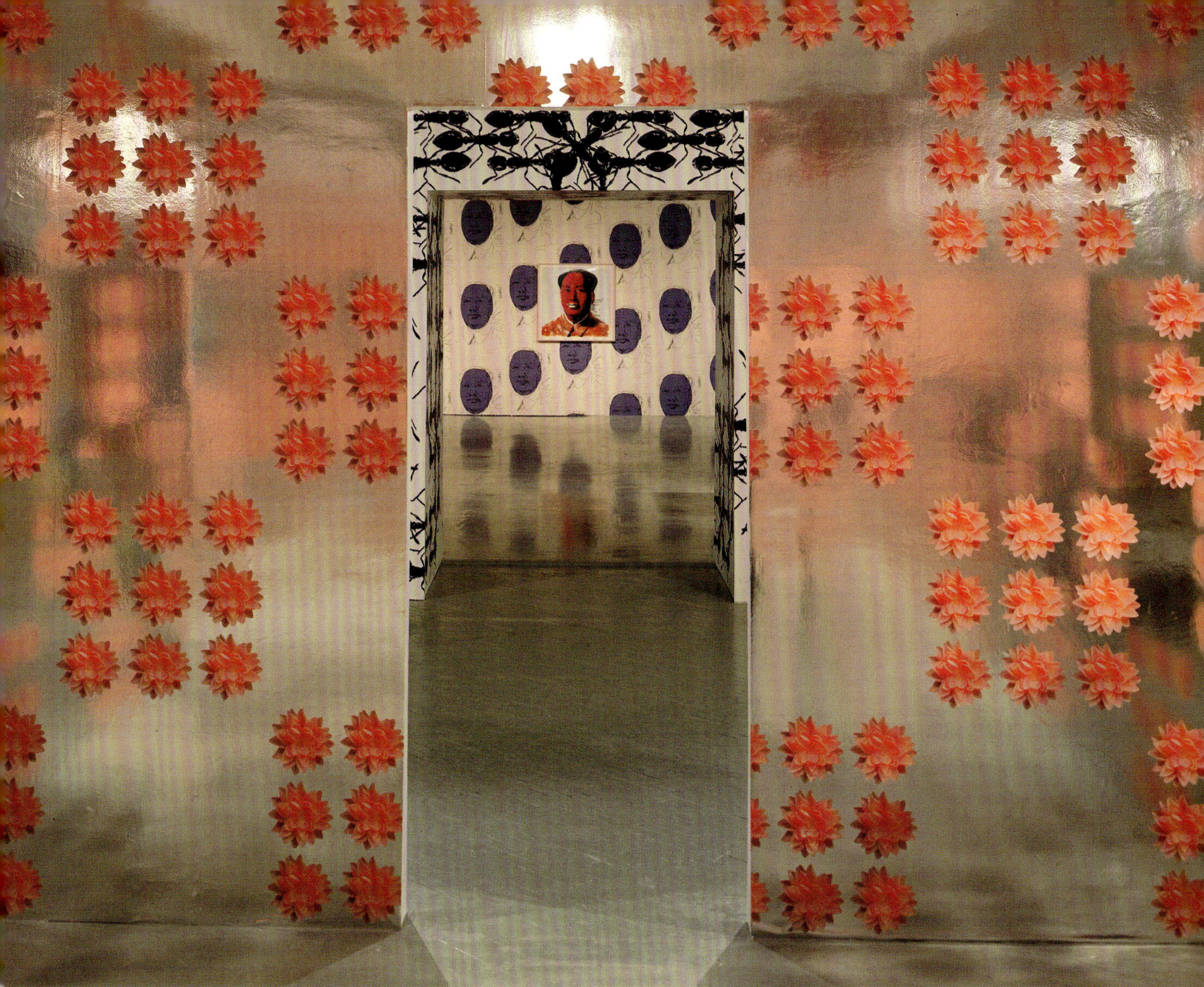

Virgil Marti (foreground), Peter Kogler (middle ground), and Andy Warhol (background) at FWM

Sadly, no patron ever came forward to acquire the unforgettable work on its own terms, whatever they might be understood to be.[12] Never mind that Warhol had opted to hand over the production process to a commercial fabricator. Since this wallpapered room would be destroyed upon de-installation, how could it be handled as art for the market or museum? Could a collector stockpile enough extra rolls of the *Cow Wallpaper* to insure its availability as needed forever? Storage and re-installation problems aside, was the work as a whole conceived as something unique or as something more like an unlimited edition available to anyone purchasing sufficient rolls of wallpaper for future use?

First acclaimed as an advertising artist, Warhol seemed determined to eradicate the distinctions between "commercial" art and "museum" art after he began to make paintings and sculptures for gallery display around 1960. To this end he created paintings of everyday items bearing images: dollar bills, comics, newspapers and magazines, merchandise packaging, and so on. His *Cow Wallpaper* is just this sort of product, except that its prestige was considerably enhanced upon display as the "content" of an art-gallery exhibition. In truth, Warhol's wallpaper would look as out-of-place in a home as in a gallery. With its garish colors and simple reiterated motif, the printed paper little resembles a professionally

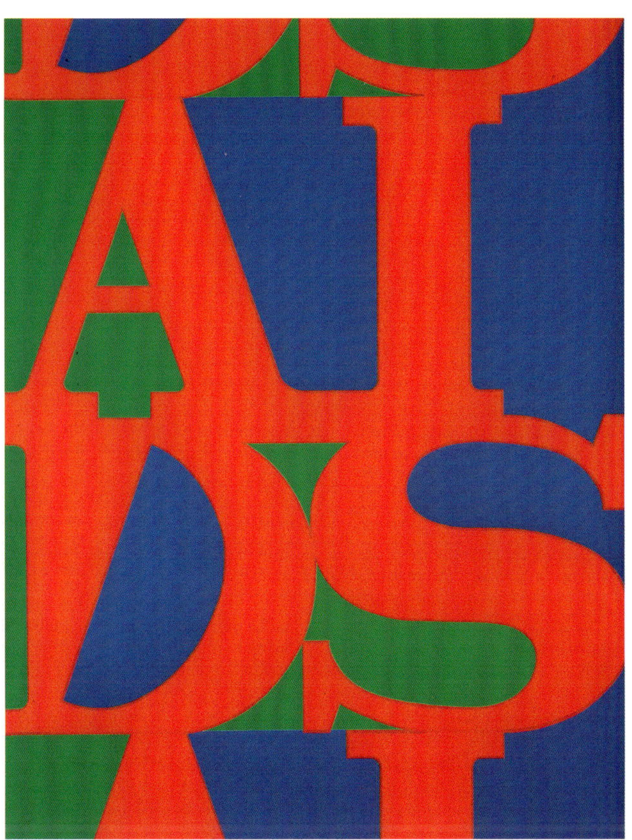

ABOVE: General Idea (collaborative group formed in 1969), *AIDS Wallpaper*, 1989, hand screenprint on paper. Courtesy of AA Bronson

FACING PAGE: Virgil Marti at FWM, *Bullies*, 1992/2001, hand screenprint with fluorescent inks and rayon flock on Tyvek (synthetic sheeting). Collection of The Fabric Workshop and Museum

designed product, relating instead to 1960s Warhol prints showing nearly identical sequential images from rolls of motion-picture film (by this time Warhol was making his own underground movies). Warhol eventually used *Cow Wallpaper* in its traditional role as a background for the display of his own paintings, but as presented in 1966, it was a background become foreground. It could also be considered an absurdist theater setting à la Alfred Jarry awaiting the arrival of its cast of characters, a sort of Pop Happening with the gallery visitors as unwitting performers.

One of the hallmarks of 1960s New York art was the integration of the display wall as a component in many large works. This is the case with the light-bulb sculptures that Dan Flavin began to make in 1963 (*alternate diagonals of March 2, 1964*, consisting of red and yellow bulbs, thus in part anticipating Warhol's *Cow Wallpaper*).[13] William Anastasi took the wall to task in a variety of 1966 works exhibited the following year at Dwan Gallery, New York. Notable among them are *Trespass*, the meticulous removal of a section of the paper skin of the gallery's Sheetrock wall; and *Six Sites*, photographic images of the gallery walls silkscreened at 9:10 scale onto canvases installed on the very walls they represent. Gordon Matta-Clark had a similar interest in deconstructing walls, not to mention buildings, and documenting it artistically. In 1972, Matta-Clark created an installation entitled *Wallspaper* at the 112 Greene Street gallery, and the following year he published an artist's book of photographed wallpaper from a tenement undergoing demolition.

Sol LeWitt's drawings, first exhibited in 1969 at the Paula Cooper Gallery, New York, were the climax of such works. Covering the entire wall as wallpaper would, these are to be realized by any draftsperson according to the artist's written description, such as: *Wall Drawing 358: A 12" (30 cm) Grid Covering the Wall. Within Each 12" (30 cm) Square, One Arc from the Corner. (The direction of the arcs and their placement are determined by the draftsman).* By relinquishing personal responsibility for the physical execution of these works, LeWitt overcame the drawbacks of traditional wallpaper art. The work's owner might remove, store, and reinstall any wall drawing with relatively few complications, since all that is needed are the instructions. Each new incarnation would be slightly different, as each performance of a musical score is uniquely expressive of the interpretative capacities of the performers, yet it remains the composer's art.

Emerging West Coast conceptual artist John Baldessari immediately seized upon the absurd humor of the situation. In 1971, Baldessari instructed students at the Nova Scotia College of Art and Design to cover a gallery's walls with the phrase,

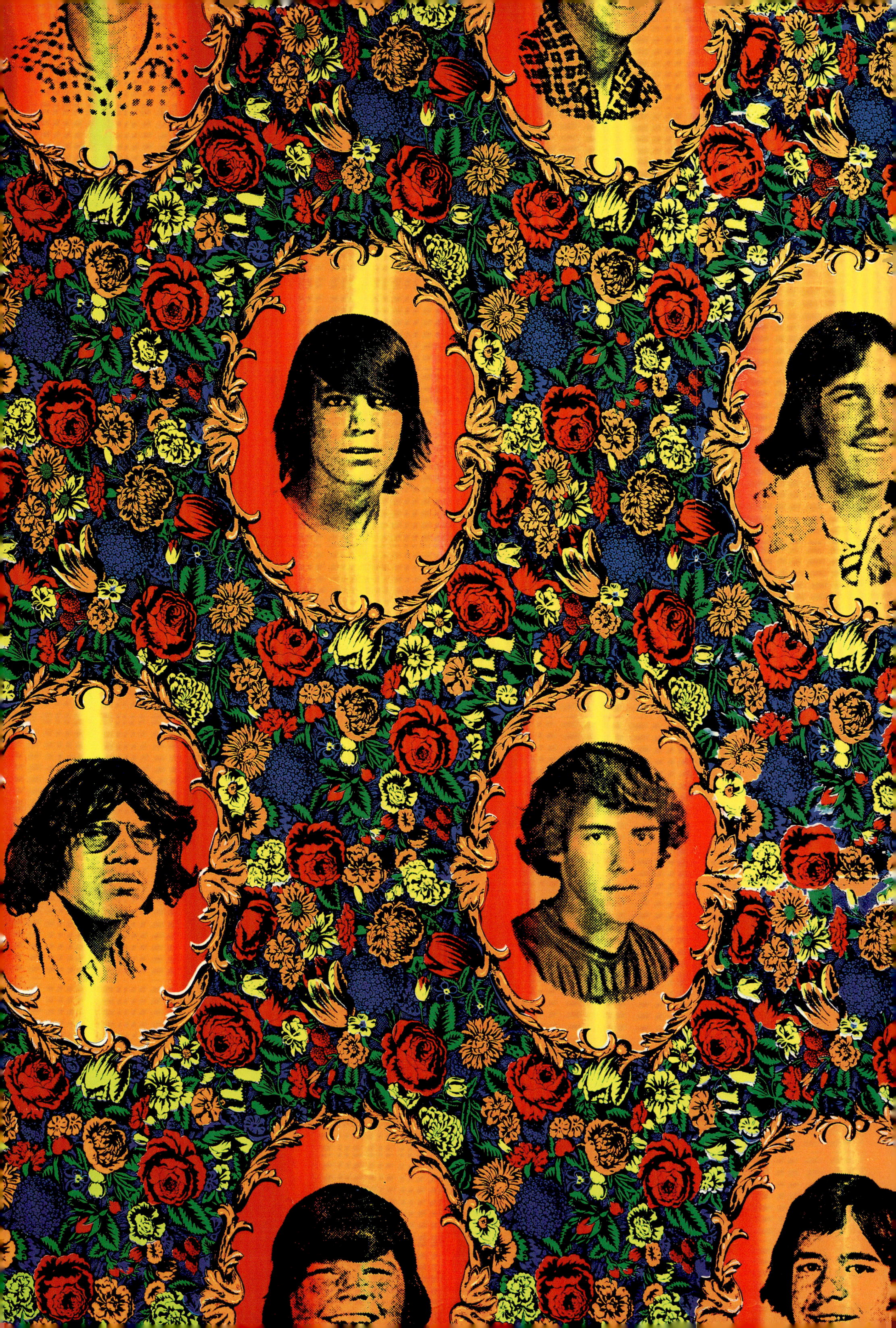

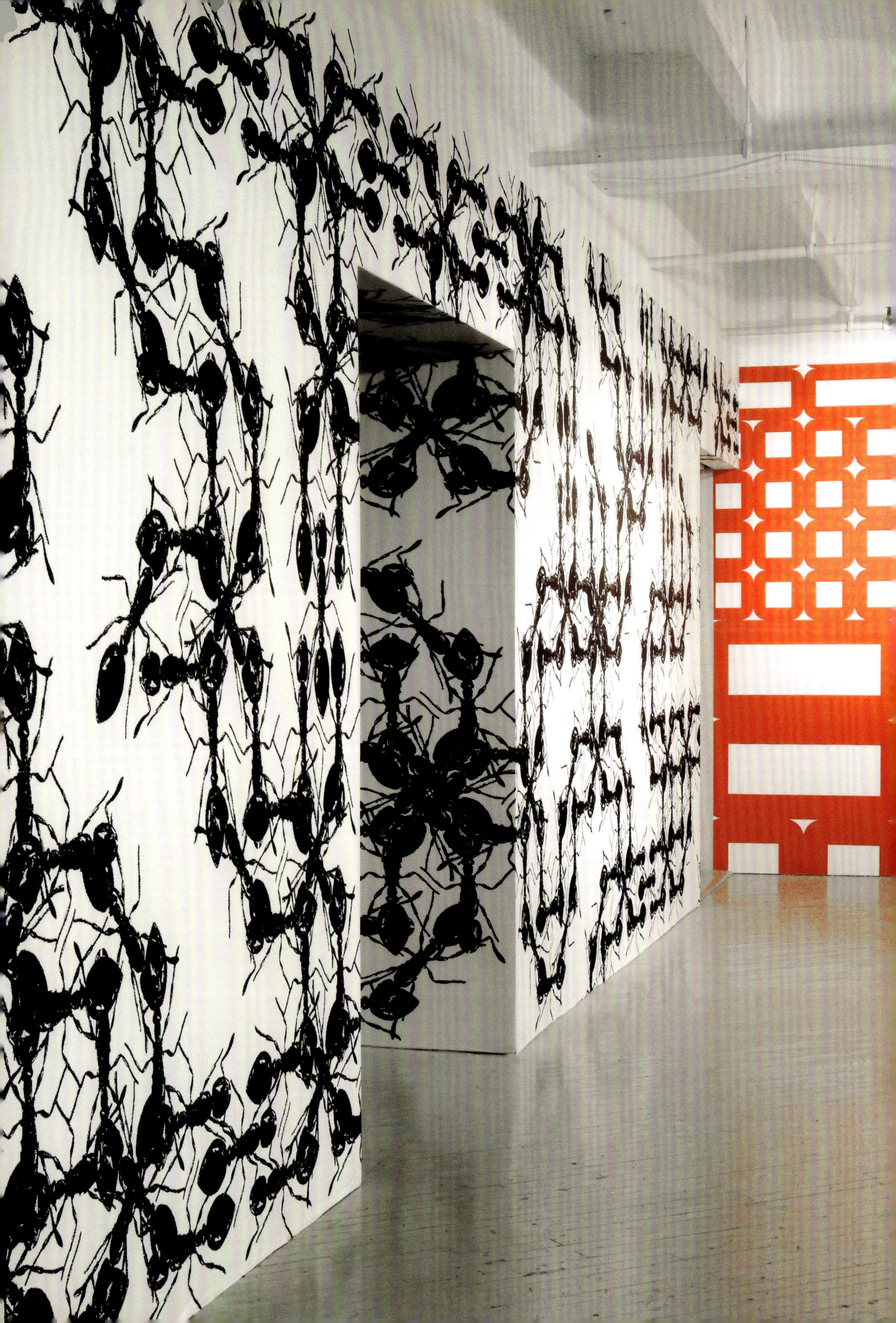

"I will not make any more boring art." Partly a respectful parody of LeWitt's deadpan written instructions for the generation of artworks by assistants, Baldessari's work is also a satirical commentary on the sorts of language art applied directly to gallery walls by Mel Bochner, Joseph Kossuth, Lawrence Wiener, and many others beginning in the mid-1960s. In 2000, Baldessari finally realized *"I Will Not Make Any More Boring Art"* as actual wallpaper.

Wall and wallpaper art have had a wide variety of embodiments worldwide, starting no later than 1959, when Austrian painter Friedrich Hundertwasser and his collaborators covered the walls of the Hamburg art school with an endless spiral. In Paris at the Salon de la jeune peinture in 1967, Daniel Buren, Olivier Mosset, Michel Parmentier, and Niele Toroni presented works with the sort of simple patterning more familiar in wallpaper than painting. With characteristic paradox, Buren sought to present such objects made from a particular striped awning material without reference to walls. The so-called BMPT group (an acronym based on the initials of their names) immediately gave license to Claude Viallet and the Support-Surface group, whose simply patterned works without stretchers must be taken into consideration in any brief survey of wallpaper-related art.

Warhol's underground films and the experimental ways of projecting them seemingly encouraged such pioneering artists as Michael Heizer and Dennis Oppenheim. By no later than 1970, they began to exhibit environments of what might be called "projected wallpaper," using photographs, film loops, or videotape to produce wall-scale images.[14] Such projected wall/wallpaper art took on futuristic overtones around 1990 with the advent of cyberspace and home computers. Not by chance, the wealth of screensaver graphics for computer monitors in rest mode are called "wallpapers." Monumental video "wallpapers" consisting of hundreds of adjacent video screens now often dominate festival venues and corporate commercial displays from the Seoul Olympic Games to the Venice Biennale. Of course, the most brilliant advocate of this new public art type is Nam June Paik. Increasingly, blockbuster films such as *The Matrix Reloaded*, 2003, incorporate wall displays as originated by Paik to symbolize a brave new technological world with a constant kaleidoscopic panorama of background images.

Issues of technological décor and Pre-Raphaelite pattern aside, the most important wallpaper art of the last twenty-five years deals with background as moral statement. Adrian Piper made a 1977 installation consisting of a small room (5 x 5 x 7 feet) wallpapered with photographic images of racial suffering stamped over with the words "Not A Performance." A spectator taking a seat in this environment, entitled *Art for the Artworld, Surface Pattern*, 1977 (Private collection), is temporarily imprisoned with his/her awareness of ongoing social injustice. Piper's intense room set an important precedent for many memorable wallpaper-

FACING PAGE: Peter Kogler and Jim Isermann (l. to r.) at FWM. Kogler, *Untitled*, 1992, screenprint on paper. Courtesy of the artist; Isermann, *Vega*, 1999, thermal die-cut vinyl. Courtesy of the artist and Richard Telles Fine Art, Los Angeles

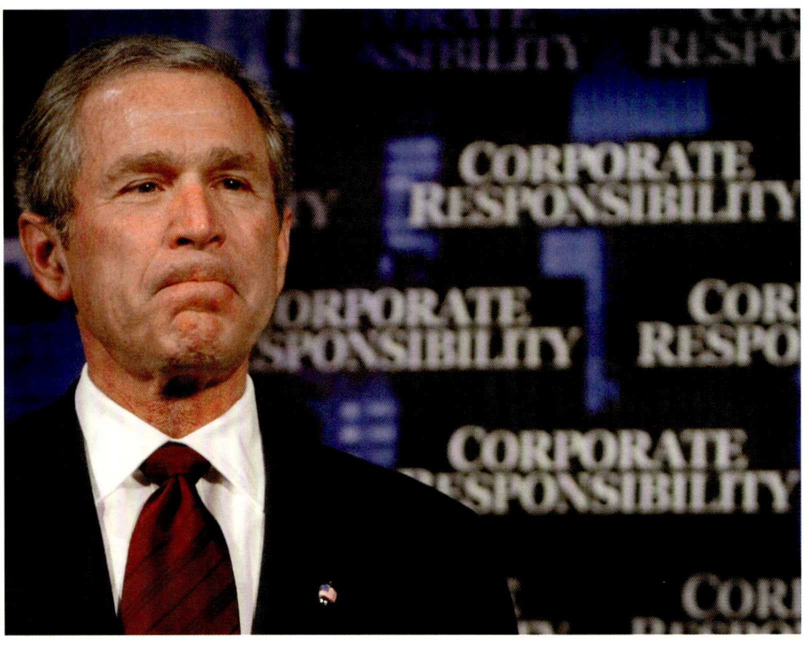

ABOVE: Photograph of President George Bush with "wallpaper"-style backdrop from "Watch His Back" in *Time*, vol. 160, no. 5 (July 29, 2002), p. 15. Courtesy of Reuters Media. Image by Larry Downing, July 9, 2002

FACING PAGE: Carrie Mae Weems at FWM, *The Apple of Adam's Eye* (folding screen), 1993, pigment and silk embroidery on cotton sateen, Australian lacewood. Created in collaboration with The Fabric Workshop and Museum. *Looking High and Low* (wallpaper), from the "Africa Series," 1993, screenprint on paper. Collection of The Fabric Workshop and Museum.

art pieces. Perhaps best known is the 1988 AIDS environment wallpapered with AIDS posters by General Idea. Alluding to Robert Indiana's famous LOVE painting (Indianapolis Museum of Art), 1966, General Idea created a bold pattern of the acronym for Acquired Immune Deficiency Syndrome, thus proposing that it should be both fashionable and compellingly necessary to address the most challenging horrors of our times. Associations of unobtrusive domestic comfort notwithstanding, wallpaper has the capacity to make any message numbingly present.

In 1989, Robert Gober began to use similar politically charged wallpaper components in his installations, starting with *Male and Female Genital Wallpaper* and *Hanging Man/Sleeping Man*, both predicated on the need to confront taboo issues that define self and other in our society. The sort of repetition inherent in wallpaper design is most often associated with boredom, but in works by General Idea, Gober, Marti, and Piper, the multiplication of ominous images is riveting, no matter how painful. Marti has transformed wallpaper into a medium of gothic self-awareness by framing sweet-seeming photographic images of boys as poisonous flowers of evil in his *Bullies* wall covering of 1992/2001. More recently, the long-standing notion that wallpaper adds warmth to domestic settings has been questioned by a growing number of younger artists. Christine Tarkowski makes dot designs on wallpaper sheets by shooting bullets through them.

Now, at the outset of the twenty-first century, wallpaper art has become ubiquitous in our propagandistic marketing culture. Reporting on messages such as "Strengthening Our Economy" that appear as surface-design pattern backdrops to underline the message of every political speech, *Time* magazine stated last July that the American government has "made a habit of visual message bearing, regularly wallpapering the President's backdrop with the official theme of the day."[15] In art and in public life, twenty-first-century scale is intended to be all encompassing, wall-to-wall and floor-to-ceiling, like wallpaper.

I wish to extend my thanks to William Anastasi, Dove Bradshaw, Virginia Dwan, James Faulkner, Ruth Fine, Elizabeth Glassman, John G. Hanhardt, Walter Hopps, Thomas McEvilley, Gerald Nordland, Michael Rooks, Robert Rosenblum, Christine Tarkowski, John Vinci, and Gabriel Weisberg.

1 Marilyn Oliver Hapgood, *Wallpaper and the Artist, From Dürer to Warhol*. New York: 1992.

2 Lesley Hoskins, ed., *The Papered Wall: History, Pattern, Technique*. London: 1994.

3 For a survey of the documentation see Mario Praz, *An Illustrated History of Interior Decoration from Pompeii to Art Nouveau*. London: 1964 (ed. 1982); and Charlotte Gere, *Nineteenth-Century Decoration: The Art of the Interior*. New York: 1989.

4 Quoted in Joseph Masheck, "The Carpet Paradigm: Critical Prolegomena to a Theory of Flatness," *Arts*, vol. 51, no. 1 (September 1976), pp. 82-109.

5 Meyer Schapiro, *Paul Cézanne*. New York: 1963, p. 52.

6 Quoted in *The Art of Paul Gauguin*. Washington, DC: 1988, p. xx.

7 See Gloria Groom, *Beyond the Easel: Decorative Paintings by Bonnard, Vuillard, Denis and Roussel, 1890-1930*. Chicago: 2001.

8 Gabriel P. Weisberg, *Art Nouveau Bing, Paris Style 1900*. New York: 1986.

9 John Richardson, *A Life of Picasso, Volume II: 1907-1917*. New York: 1996, pp. 60, 249. See Elizabeth Cowling, *Picasso, Style and Meaning*. London: 2002, pp. 240-53; and Nancy J. Troy, *Modernism and the Decorative Arts in France, Art Nouveau to Le Corbusier*. New Haven and London: 1991, passim.

10 Mary Abbe Staniszewski, *The Power of Display, A History of Exhibition Installations at the Museum of Modern Art*. Cambridge (Massachusetts) and London (England): 1998, pp. 16-21.

11 See *Apocalyptic Wallpaper: Robert Gober, Abigail Lane, Virgil Marti, and Andy Warhol*. Columbus: 1997, pp. 8, 13.

12 Not counting Holly Solomon. In 1966, she wanted Warhol to use a photograph of herself (rather than the cow design) to make a wall paper for her home. As a dealer, Solomon would subsequently specialize in Pattern and Decoration artists. Perhaps inadvertently, but certainly ironically, her book *Living With Art*, 1988, authored with Alexandra Anderson, documents how taboo wallpaper remains in contemporary interiors. There is none visible in any of the rooms represented in her survey of collectors' homes.

13 For an overview of the genre, see Jörg Schellmann, ed., *Wall Works, Site-Specific Wall Installations*. New York: 1999.

14 See Chrissie Iles, *Into the Light, The Projected Image in American Art 1964-1977*. New York: 2001.

15 "Watch His Back" in *Time*, vol. 160, no. 5 (July 29, 2002), p. 15.

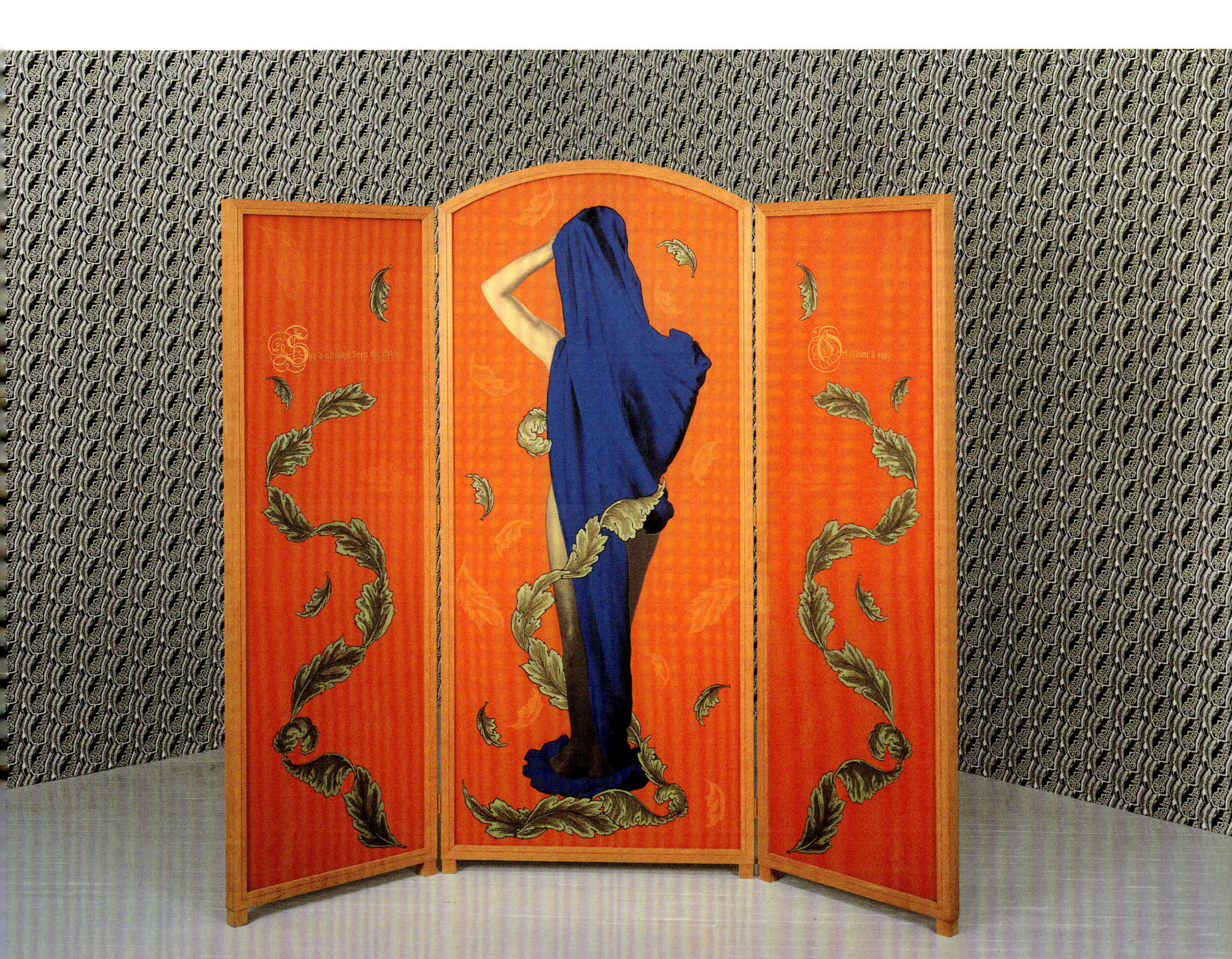

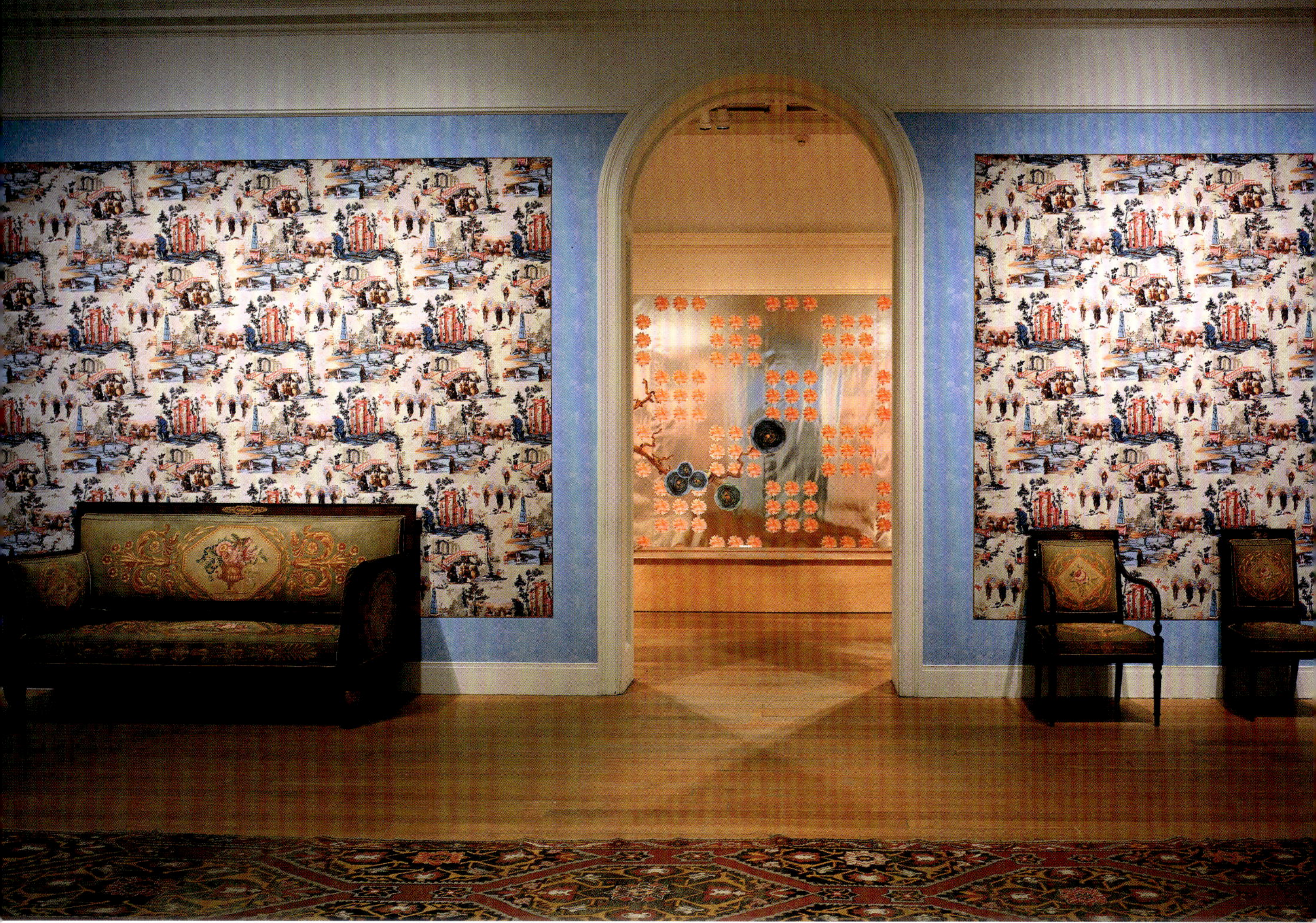

on the wall

wallpaper by contemporary artists

Checklist of the Exhibition

The RISD Museum, Providence
February 7–April 20, 2003

Dimensions are given in inches unless otherwise indicated: height (or length) precedes width precedes depth. The term screenprint has been used to describe the technique also known as silkscreen and related processes.

Ann Agee
American, b. 1959

Jello Yellow Calico, 1995
Gouache on rice paper, 180 x 49

Man in Plaid Jacket with Paper Bag, 1997
Porcelain, 9 1/2 h.

Woman with Camera and Pink Skirt, 1998
Porcelain, 7 1/2 h.

Home Birth #2, 2001
Porcelain, 8 1/2 x 12 1/2 x 8 1/2

Woman with Polka-Dot Tank Top and Red Plaid Scarf, 2002
Porcelain, 8 1/2 h.

Woman with Yellow Flowered Dress, 2002
Porcelain, 8 3/4 h.

Courtesy of the artist

John Baldessari
American, b. 1931

Wallpaper for 4 RMS W VU:

Potato/Lightbulb – Blue, 1996

Ear/Pretzel – Pink, 1996

Clock/Pizza – Turquoise, 1996

Nose/Popcorn – Yellow/Green, 1996

Digital color prints on paper, sheet 39 3/8 x 22 3/8
Courtesy of the artist and Marian Goodman Gallery, New York

I Will Not Make Any More Boring Art (wallpaper), 1971/2000
Screenprint on paper, partial roll: 79 1/2 x 27
Courtesy of the artist and Printed Matter, New York

Matthew Benedict
American, b. 1968

The House of the Seven Gables, 1998
Gouache on wood, overall: 7′ x 7′11″
Courtesy of the artist and Alexander and Bonin, New York

Brian Chippendale
American, b. 1973

The Only House I Can Afford in Providence, 2003
Hand screenprint on newspaper on wood with collaged hand-screenprinted cutouts, overall: 9′ h. x 7′ diam. approx.
Courtesy of the artist

Adam Cvijanovic
American, b. 1960

Space Park, 2003
Flasche, acrylic, and latex on Tyvek (synthetic sheeting), overall: 21′ x 18 1/2′ approx.
Courtesy of the artist and Bellwether Gallery, Brooklyn

General Idea
(collaborative group formed in 1969)

AA Bronson (b. Michael Tims)
Canadian, b. 1946

Felix Partz (b. Ronald Gabe)
Canadian, 1945–94

Jorge Zontal (b. Slobodan Saia-Levy)
Canadian, b. Italy, 1944–94

AIDS Wallpaper, 1989
Hand screenprint on paper, roll: 180 x 27; overall: 12′ x 9′ approx.

Courtesy of AA Bronson

Robert Gober
American, b. 1954
Male and Female Genital Wallpaper, 1989
Hand screenprint on paper, rolls A and B: 180 x 24 each
Courtesy of the artist

Rodney Graham
Canadian, b. 1949
City Self/Country Self (wallpaper), 2001
Hand screenprint on paper, roll: 180 x 27
Courtesy of Donald Young Gallery, Chicago

Renée Green
American, b. 1959
Mise-en-Scène: Commemorative Toile, 1992
Hand screenprint on paper-backed cotton sateen, partial roll: 101¾ x 52
Created in collaboration with The Fabric Workshop and Museum. Collection of The Fabric Workshop and Museum

Jenny Holzer
American, b. 1950
Inflammatory Essays, 1979–82
Offset print on paper, sheet: 17 x 17; overall: 12′ x 8′6″ approx.
Courtesy of the artist and Cheim & Read, New York

Jim Isermann
American, b. 1955
Untitled (0900), 2000
Plotter-cut Mylar, sheet: 24 x 24; overall: 21′ x 23′ approx.
Courtesy of the artist and Richard Telles Fine Art, Los Angeles

Virgil Marti
American, b. 1962
Lotus Room, 2003
Room installation with wallpaper and digital decals, 12′6″ x 31′7″ x 19′2″ approx. (irregular)
Lotus Wallpaper, 2003
Hand screenprint on Mylar, roll: 50 w.
Created in collaboration with the RISD Printmaking Department, The RISD Museum, and The Fabric Workshop and Museum.
Courtesy of the artist

Jane Masters
American, b. England, 1962
Groovy: Version 4, 2003
Hand screenprint on paper, sheet: 20 x 20; overall: 12′ x 8′ approx.
Courtesy of the artist

Takashi Murakami
Japanese, b. 1962
Jellyfish Eyes, 2002
Hand screenprint on paper, roll: 180 x 27; overall: 12′ x 7′9″ approx.
Courtesy of Marianne Boesky Gallery, New York

Joan Nelson
American, b. 1958
Wallpaper, 1991
Hand screenprint on paper, roll: 180 x 30
Collection of The RISD Museum, Gift of A/D Gallery 1993.057

Paul Noble
English, b. 1963
nobnest zed, 2002
Offset print on paper, sheet: 19 x 27½; overall: 9′5″ x 5′1″ approx.
Courtesy of *nest* magazine and nest products

Jorge Pardo
American, b. Cuba, 1963
Untitled, 1999
Hand screenprint on paper-backed cotton sateen, roll: 54 w.
Created in collaboration with The Fabric Workshop and Museum. Collection of Marion Boulton Stroud

FACING PAGE: Francesco Simeti (foreground) and Virgil Marti (background) at RISD. Simeti, *Arabian Nights*, 2003, wallpapered room with suite of furniture and rug; *Arabian Nights* and *Are You Ready?* wallpaper and border: digital print on paper. Created in collaboration with The RISD Museum. Courtesy of the artist and Galleria Massimo Minini, Brescia. Marti, *Lotus Room*, 2003, wallpaper: hand screenprint on Mylar, digital decals. Created in collaboration with the Printmaking Department, Rhode Island School of Design, The RISD Museum, and The Fabric Workshop and Museum. Courtesy of the artist

BELOW: Christine Tarkowski, Ann Agee, Rodney Graham, Renée Green, Joan Nelson, Carrie Mae Weems, General Idea, Takashi Murakami (l. to r. on walls), and John Baldessari (in case) at RISD

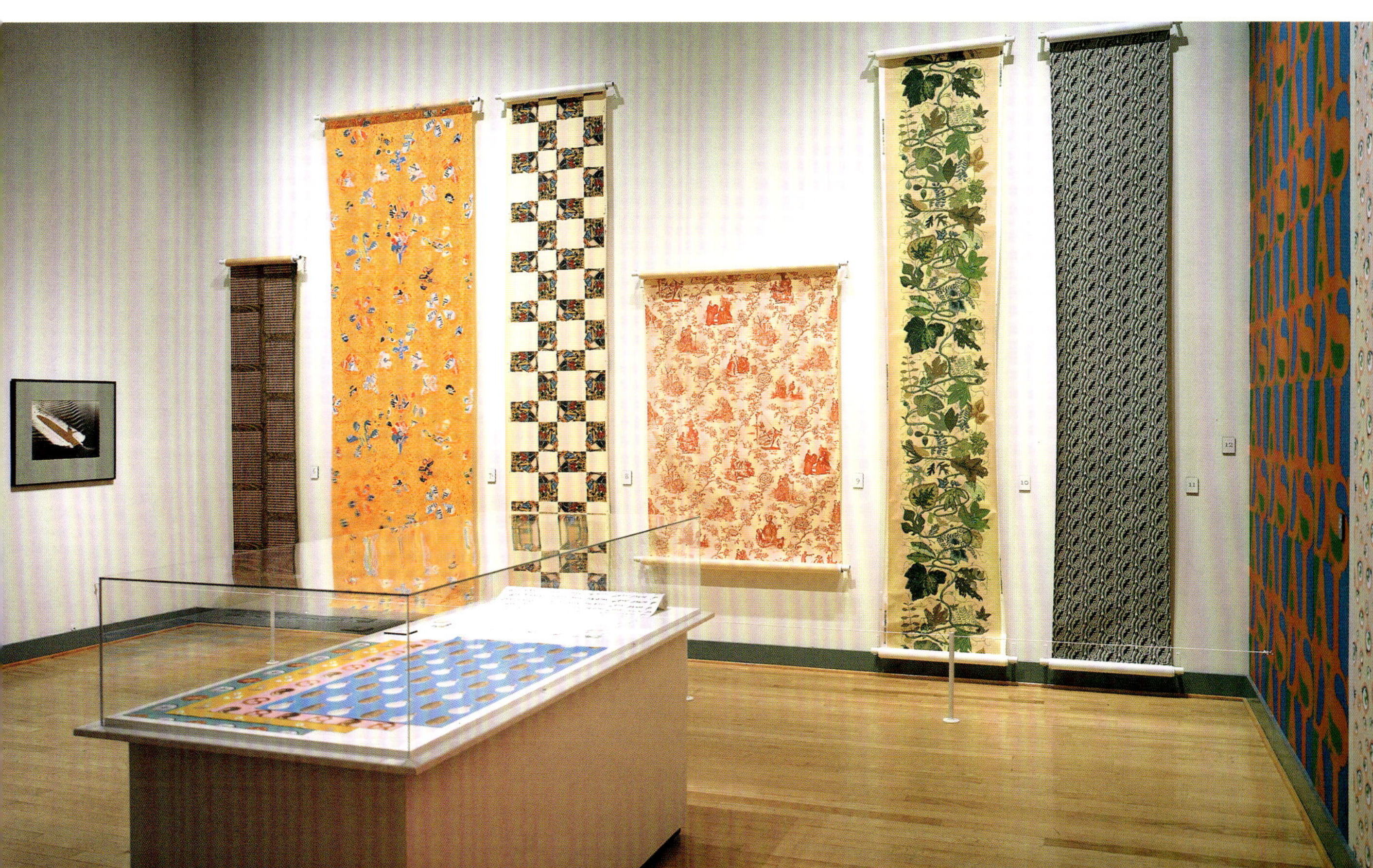

Francesco Simeti
Italian and American, b. 1968

Arabian Nights, 2003
Wallpapered room with suite of furniture and rug, 12′6″ x 31′7″ x 19′2″ approx. (irregular)

Arabian Nights and *Are You Ready?* (wallpapers), 2003
Digital print on paper, roll: 19 5/8 w.
Created in collaboration with The RISD Museum. Courtesy of the artist and Galleria Massimo Minini, Brescia

Jean-Baptiste Reveillon
French, 1725-1811
Imitation of a Toile de Jouy, 1789
(source for *Arabian Nights* wallpaper)
Woodblock on paper, 23 1/4 x 18 7/8
Collection of The RISD Museum,
Mary B. Jackson Fund 34.888

French
Suite of Furniture (6 armchairs, 4 side chairs, and settee), ca. 1900
Mahogany, mahogany veneer, gilt brass, and wool/silk tapestry weave (upholstery)
Collection of The RISD Museum,
Gift of Mrs. Harold Brown 37.127-.138

Do-Ho Suh
Korean, b. 1962

Who Am We? (multi), 2000
Color offset print on paper, sheet: 24 x 36; overall: 9′9″ x 11′5″ approx.
Courtesy of the artist and Lehmann Maupin Gallery, New York

Christine Tarkowski
American, b. 1967

Exposed Stud/Nuclear Sub from the "Architectural Targets" series, 1998
gouache on ink-jet print on paper,
16 x 22: hand screenprint on paper, roll: 117 x 24
Courtesy of the artist

Andy Warhol
American, 1928–87

Cow Wallpaper, 1966; refabricated for the Andy Warhol Museum, Pittsburgh, 1994
Hand screenprint on paper, roll: 180 x 28; overall: 17′5″- 9′5″ (h. varies) x 38′6″ approx.
Courtesy of the Andy Warhol Museum, Pittsburgh. © 2003 Andy Warhol Foundation for the Visual Arts/ARS, New York

Carrie Mae Weems
American, b. 1953

Looking High and Low (wallpaper), from the "Africa Series," 1993
Hand screenprint on paper, roll: 180 x 26 1/2
Courtesy of P.P.O.W. Gallery, New York

William Wegman
American, b. 1943

Alphabet Border (wallpaper), 1993
Hand screenprint on paper, roll: 13 1/2 x 360
Courtesy of the artist and A/D Gallery, New York

FACING PAGE, ABOVE: Jorge Pardo, *Untitled* (wallpaper), 1999, hand screenprint on paper-backed cotton sateen. Created in collaboration with The Fabric Workshop and Museum. Collection of The Fabric Workshop and Museum

FACING PAGE, BELOW: Jorge Pardo, *Untitled* (video lounge at FWM), 1999; wallpaper: hand screenprint on paper-backed cotton sateen; fabric: hand screenprint on linen and Swiss cotton; furniture, lamps, cork floor, and birch plywood ceiling. Created in collaboration with The Fabric Workshop and Museum. Collection of The Fabric Workshop and Museum

Historic Wallpaper from the Collection of The RISD Museum

Attrib. to Père Boulard
French, active Rouen, 1730-70
Two blue and white Dominos with floral sprays, ca. 1750
Printed in ink on paper, 17 x 13 1/4; 16 3/4 x 13 1/2
Mary B. Jackson Fund 34.867, 34.868

Chinese, Qing dynasty (1644-1911)
Court Scene, ca. 1770
Hand painted on rice paper, 54 1/4 x 49 1/8
Mary B. Jackson Fund 34.862

Attrib. to Jean-Baptiste Pillement
French, 1728-1808
Wallpaper panel, ca. 1780
Block print on paper, 67 1/4 x 16
Mary B. Jackson Fund 34.875

Etienne de Lavallée-Poussin, designer
French, 1735-1802
Jean-Baptiste Réveillon, manufacturer
French, 1725-1811
Wallpaper panel, ca. 1790
Printed and hand painted in tempera on paper, 51 x 15 3/4
Mary B. Jackson Fund 34.959

Huard & Chasset
Paris, France, early 20th century
Jardins de Palais Royal, ca. 1805-10 (original design), reprinted 1924
Block print on paper, 74 x 56 7/8
Mary B. Jackson Fund 34.952

French
Probably Joseph Dufour and Company; or Zuber and Company; manufacturer
Paris, France, fl. 1804-36; or Rixheim, France, 1790-present
Base and capital, ca. 1810-20
Block print on laid paper, base: 7 9/16 x 6 13/16; capital: 9 3/8 x 6 7/16
Mary B. Jackson Fund 34.1125, 34.1126

Xavier Mader, designer
French, 1789-1830
Joseph Dufour and Company, manufacturer
Paris, France, fl. 1804-36
Judgment of Paris, Trophy with Bust of Homer, and *Trophy with Bust of a Woman*, from "The Galerie Mythologique" series, 1814
Block print on paper; 41 3/4 x 83 1/2; 41 3/4 x 25 5/16; 41 3/4 x 25 5/16
Mary B. Jackson Fund 34.996, 34.995, 34.997

Eugène Ehrmann, Georges Zipélius, and Joseph Fuchs, designers
French
Zuber and Company, manufacturer
Rixheim, France, 1790-present
El Dorado, designed ca. 1848, produced ca. 1890-1900
Block print on wove paper, each panel: 126 x 22
Gift of Richard and Inge Chafee in Memory of Zechariah and Mary Dexter Chafee and Their Daughter, Mary 1994.101.1-.2

Attrib. to Tomita
Chinese, mid-19th century
Wallpaper panel
Hand painted on paper, 53 3/4 x 22 3/4
Museum Purchase 49.135a,b

British or American
Wallpaper fragment, ca. 1880
Printed with metallic powder on paper, 26 x 19 3/4
Gift of N. David Barry Scotti 2002.39.1.1

British
Wallpaper fragment, 1882
Embossed and printed on paper, 29 x 12
Gift of N. David Barry Scotti 2002.39.4.1

British
Wallpaper fragment, 1882
Embossed and printed on paper, 11 1/4 x 11 1/4
Gift of N. David Barry Scotti 2002.39.14

Dagobert Peche, designer
Austrian, 1887-1923
Flammersheim & Steinmann, manufacturer
Cologne, Germany, ca. 1919-60
Spitze (*Lace*), 1920
Roller print on wove paper, 25 1/2 x 22
Gift of Norman Herreshoff 84.235

Alexander Calder, designer
American, 1898-1976
Laverne Originals, manufacturer
New York, New York, founded 1938
Splotchy, 1949
Screenprint on paper, 372 x 55 1/2
Abby Rockefeller Mauzé Fund 82.098

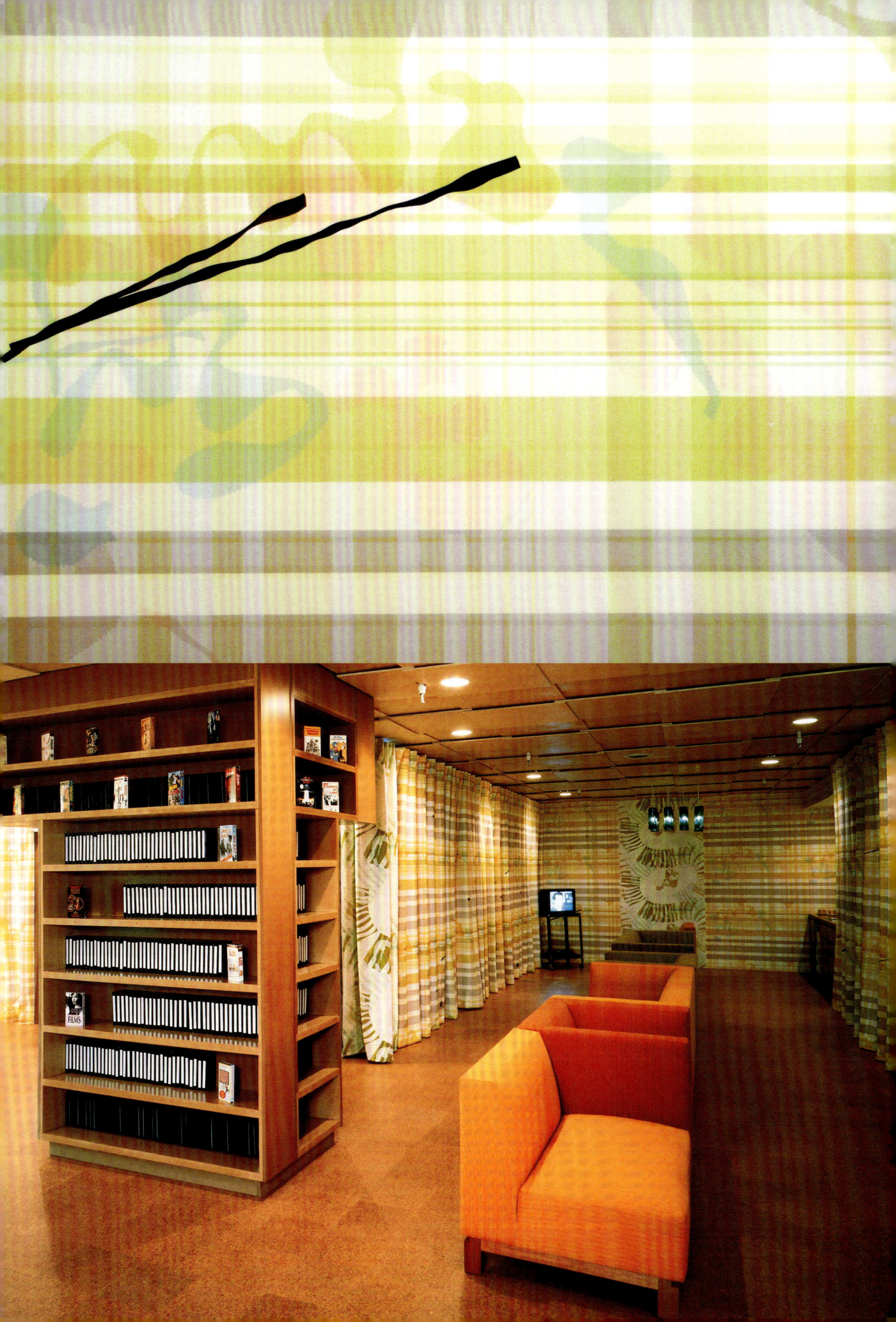

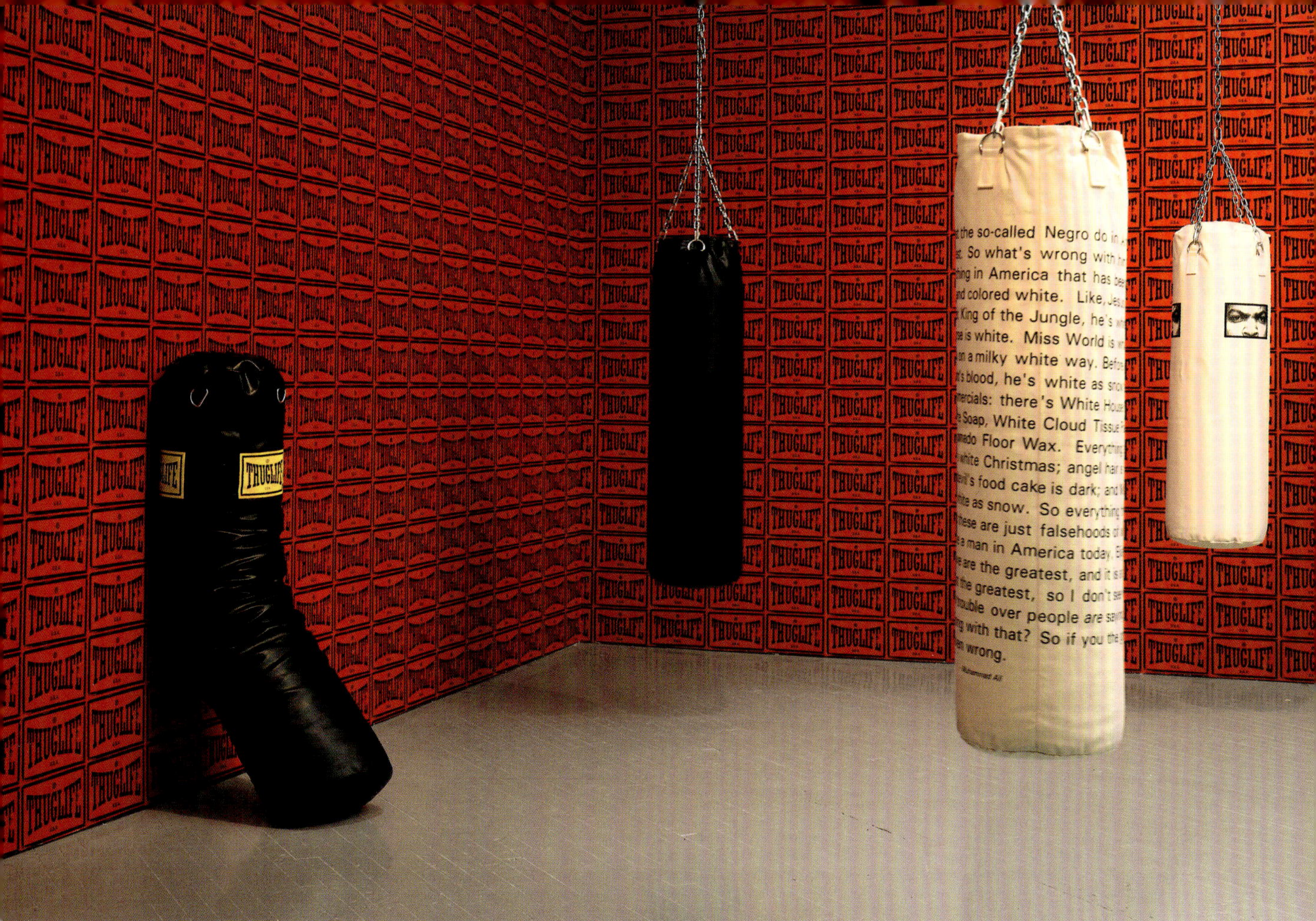

on the wall

wallpaper and tableau

Checklist of the Exhibition

The Fabric Workshop and Museum, Philadelphia
May 9–September 13, 2003

Dimensions are given in inches unless otherwise indicated: height (or length) precedes width precedes depth. The term screenprint has been used to describe the technique also known as silkscreen and related processes.

John Baldessari
American, b. 1931

Wallpaper for 4 RMS W VU:

Potato/Lightbulb – Blue, 1996

Ear/Pretzel – Pink, 1996

Clock/Pizza – Turquoise, 1996

Nose/Popcorn – Yellow/Green, 1996

Digital color prints on paper, sheet 39 3/8 x 22 3/8
Courtesy of the artist and Marian Goodman Gallery, New York

I Will Not Make Any More Boring Art, 1971/2000
Screenprint on paper, partial roll: 79 1/2 x 27
Courtesy of the artist, Printed Matter, New York, and The RISD Museum

Mike Bidlo
American, b. 1953

R. Mutt Wallpaper, 1997/2002
Offset print on newsprint, sheet: 10 x 10; overall: 10′ x 19′8″
Printed with the assistance of The Fabric Workshop and Museum. Courtesy of the artist and Galerie Bruno Bischofberger, Zürich

Adam Cvijanovic
American, b. 1960

Backyard, 2002
Flasche, acrylic, and latex on Tyvek (synthetic sheeting), overall: 10′ x 50′ approx.
Courtesy of the artist and Bellwether Gallery, Brooklyn

Drew Dominick
American, b. 1964

Member Shots and Varmint Master, 1999
Hand screenprint on rag paper, roll: 42 w.; 25 x 33
Private collection

Nicole Eisenman
American, b. France, 1965

Gray Bar Hotel, 2003
Hand screenprint on paper-backed cotton sateen, roll: 50 w.; overall: 10′ x 31′10″
Created in collaboration with The Fabric Workshop and Museum. Collection of The Fabric Workshop and Museum

ABOVE: Glenn Ligon at FWM, *Skin Tight*, 1995 (bags) and *Untitled*, 2003 (wallpaper); bags: cotton, canvas, leather, vinyl, pigment and metal chain; wallpaper: hand screenprint on acrylic and paper. Created in collaboration with The Fabric Workshop and Museum. Collection of The Fabric Workshop and Museum

FACING PAGE: Rodney Graham, *City Self/Country Self* (wallpaper), 2001, hand screenprint on paper. Courtesy of Donald Young Gallery, Chicago

Viola Frey
American, b. 1933

Artist's Mind/Studio/World wallpaper, 1992
Hand screenprint on paper-backed cotton sateen, roll: 56 1/2 w.; overall: 10′ x 17′4″ and 10′ x 11′
Created in collaboration with The Fabric Workshop and Museum. Collection of The Fabric Workshop and Museum

Artist's Mind/Studio/World border, 1992
Hand screenprint on paper-backed cotton sateen, roll: 15 h.
overall: 1′3″ x 17′4″ and 1′3″ x 11′
Created in collaboration with The Fabric Workshop and Museum. Collection of The Fabric Workshop and Museum

World II, 2002
Ceramic, 52 diam.
Courtesy of Nancy Hoffman Gallery, New York

General Idea
(collaborative group formed in 1969)

AA Bronson (b. Michael Tims)
Canadian, b. 1946

Felix Partz (b. Ronald Gabe)
Canadian, 1945–94

Jorge Zontal (b. Slobodan Saia-Levy)
Canadian, b. Italy, 1944–94

AIDS Wallpaper, 1989
Hand screenprint on paper, partial roll: 82 x 27;
Courtesy of AA Bronson and The RISD Museum

Robert Gober
American, b. 1954

Hanging Man/Sleeping Man (wallpaper), 1989
Hand screenprint on paper, partial roll: 36 x 27
Collection of Marion Boulton Stroud

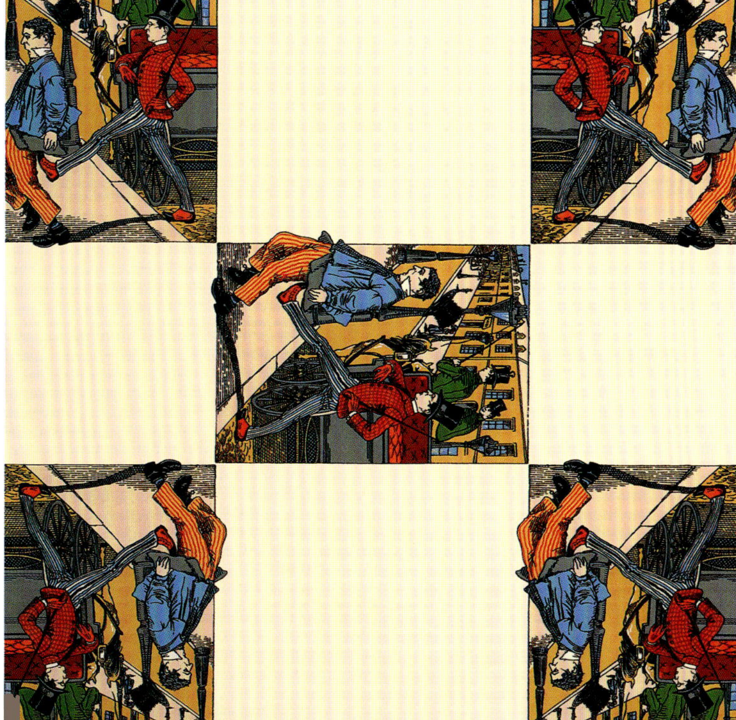

Lonnie Graham
American, b. 1954

Wallpaper from *In a Spirit House*, 1993
Hand screenprint on paper-backed cotton sateen; roll: 54 w.; partial roll: 25 x 25
Collection of The Fabric Workshop and Museum

Rodney Graham
Canadian, b. 1949

City Self/Country Self (wallpaper), 2001
Hand screenprint on paper, roll: 180 x 27;
overall: 10′ x 13′8″
Courtesy of Donald Young Gallery, Chicago

Renée Green
American, b.1959

Mise-en-Scène: Commemorative Toile, 1992
Wallpaper: hand screenprint on paper-backed cotton sateen, roll: 52 w.;
overall: 10′ x 17′4″ and 10′ x 11′
Upholstery: hand screenprint on cotton sateen, 56 1/2 w.
Created in collaboration with The Fabric Workshop and Museum. Collection of The Fabric Workshop and Museum

Richard Haas
American, b. 1936

Rose Trellis Motif from *Rose Lobby*, installed in the Home Savings Bank, Pasadena, 1990
Hand screenprint on canvas with hand painting, overall: 73 x 49
Courtesy of the artist

Trenton Doyle Hancock
American, b. 1974

Flower Bed (wallpaper), 2003
Hand screenprint on paper,
roll: 360 x 27; overall: 10′ x 35′
Courtesy the artist and James Cohan Gallery, New York

Day Carts, 2002
Graphite, acrylic, and ink on paper, 11 3/4 x 9 1/2, framed: 14 1/4 x 12
Courtesy of James Cohan Gallery, New York

New Marily, 2002
Graphite, acrylic, and ink on paper, 11 1/4 x 9 3/4, framed: 14 1/2 x 13 1/4
Courtesy of James Cohan Gallery, New York

Roy Jebef, 2002
Graphite, acrylic, and ink on paper, 11 1/4 x 9, framed: 14 1/8 x 11 1/2
Courtesy of James Cohan Gallery, New York

Horace Race, 2002
Graphite, acrylic, and ink on paper, 11 1/4 x 9, framed: 13 3/4 x 11 1/2
Courtesy of CRG Gallery, New York

Faith, 2002
Graphite, acrylic, and ink on paper, 12 x 11, framed: 14 1/2 x 13 1/4
Collection of Gregory Miller

Xanidude, 2002
Graphite, acrylic, and ink on paper, 11 1/4 x 9 1/8, framed: 13 1/2 x 11 3/8
Collection of Gregory Miller

Basilly St. Clout, 2002
Graphite, acrylic, and ink on paper, 11 1/4 x 9 1/2, framed: 13 5/8 x 12
Collection of Perry Rubenstein and Sara Fitzmaurice

Golly You're Tall, 2002
Graphite, acrylic, and ink on paper, 11 1/4 x 9 1/2, framed: 15 7/8 x 11 3/8
Collection of Perry Rubenstein and Sara Fitzmaurice

Jenny Holzer
American, b. 1950

Inflammatory Essays, 1979–82
Offset print on paper; sheet: 17 x 17;
overall: 10′ x 21′8″ and 8′ x 18′6″ x 13′6″
Courtesy of the artist and Cheim & Read, New York

Jim Isermann
American, b. 1955

Vega, 1999
Thermal die-cut vinyl, sheet: 23 1/2 x 23 1/2;
overall: 10′ x 53′9″
Courtesy of the artist and Richard Telles Fine Art, Los Angeles

Peter Kogler
Austrian, b. 1959

Untitled, 1992
Screenprint on paper, sheet: 24 x 24;
overall: 10′ x 45′4″
Courtesy of the artist

Roy Lichtenstein
American, 1923–97

Interior with Blue Floor (wallpaper), 1992
Hand screenprint on paper (5 panels), overall: 8′6 1/2″ x 12′8 3/8″ (edition 42/300)
Collection of The RISD Museum, Georgianna Sayles Aldrich Fund 1993.004

Brushstroke Chair, 1986-88
Painted wood, 70 11/16 x 18 x 27 1/4 (edition 8/12)
Courtesy of the Estate of Roy Lichtenstein

Brushstroke Ottoman, 1986–89
Painted wood, 20 3/4 x 17 3/4 x 24 (edition 9/12)
Courtesy of the Estate of Roy Lichtenstein

Glenn Ligon
American, b. 1960

Skin Tight, 1995 (punching bags) and 2003 (wallpaper)
Bags: cotton, canvas, leather, vinyl, pigment and metal chain, 45-51 h. (varies) x 13 diam. (edition of 7)
Wallpaper: hand screenprint on acrylic and paper, roll: 42 w.; overall: 10′ x 17′4″ and 10′ x 11′
Created in collaboration with The Fabric Workshop and Museum. Collection of The Fabric Workshop and Museum

Virgil Marti
American, b. 1962

Lotus Room, 2003
Hand screenprint on Mylar, digital decals, roll: 50 w.; overall: 10′ x 16′6″ (each of two walls) and 10′ x 13′2″ (each of two walls) approx.
Created in collaboration with the RISD Printmaking Department, The RISD Museum, and The Fabric Workshop and Museum.
Courtesy of the artist

Bullies, 1992/2001
Hand screenprint with fluorescent inks and rayon flock on Tyvek (synthetic sheeting), roll: 50 w.; overall: 8′ x 14′2″ x 10′
Collection of The Fabric Workshop and Museum

Beer Can Collection Mid-1970s, 1999
Hand screenprint on paper in wood frame with brass plate, 8′6″ x 13′ (edition of 6)
Courtesy of the artist

Jane Masters
American, b. England, 1962

Groovy: Version 4, 2003
Hand screenprint on paper, sheet: 20 x 20; overall: 10′ x 21′8″
Courtesy of the artist

Michael Mercil
American, b. 1954

Wallpaper from *In My Father's House: An Historical Melancholy in Two Acts, Act I: Belongings Belonging*, 2000
Hand screenprint on paper-backed cotton sateen; partial roll: 25 x 36
Collection of The Fabric Workshop and Museum

Takashi Murakami
Japanese, b. 1962

Jellyfish Eyes, 2002
Hand screenprint on paper, roll: 180 x 27; overall: 10′ x 25′7 1/2″
Courtesy of Marianne Boesky Gallery, New York

Paul Noble
English, b. 1963

nobnest zed, 2002
Offset print on paper, sheet: 19 x 27 1/2; overall: 10′ x 16′8″
Courtesy of Tim Gleason Gallery, New York, and *nest* products

BELOW: Glenn Ligon (foreground) and Rob Wynne (background) at FWM. Ligon, *Skin Tight*, 1995 (bags) and *Untitled*, 2003 (wallpaper); bags: cotton, canvas, leather, vinyl, pigment and metal chain; wallpaper: hand screenprint on acrylic and paper. Created in collaboration with The Fabric Workshop and Museum. Collection of The Fabric Workshop and Museum. Wynne, *Eyes Wallpaper*, 2003, hand screenprint on paper. Courtesy of the artist

FACING PAGE: Trenton Doyle Hancock and Viola Frey (l. to r.) at FWM. Hancock, *Flower Bed* (wallpaper), 2003, hand screenprint on paper, and eight framed drawings. Courtesy the artist and James Cohan Gallery, New York. Frey, *Artist's Mind/Studio/World* (wallpaper), 1992, hand screenprint on paper-backed cotton sateen. Created in collaboration with The Fabric Workshop and Museum. Collection of The Fabric Workshop and Museum

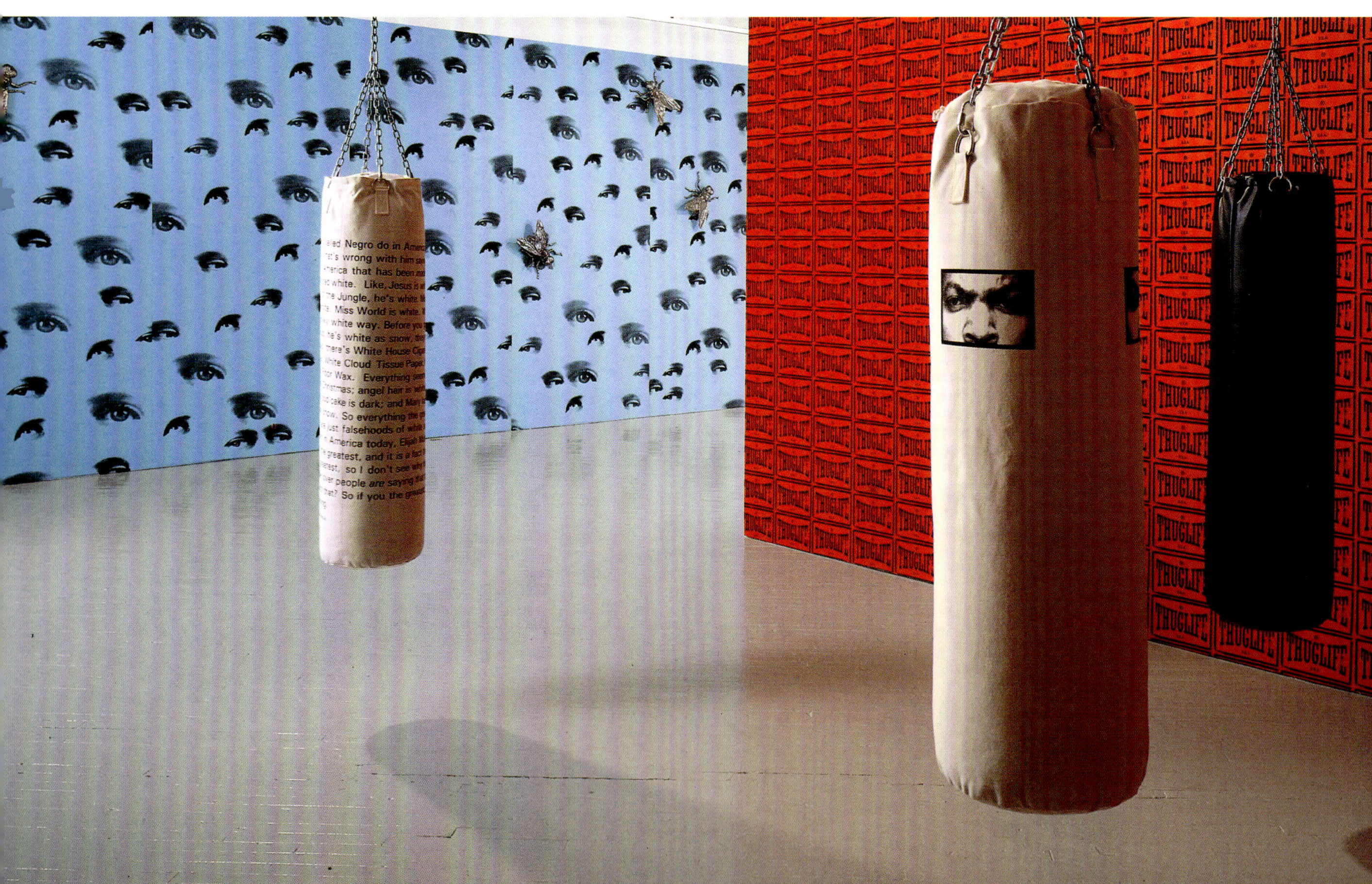

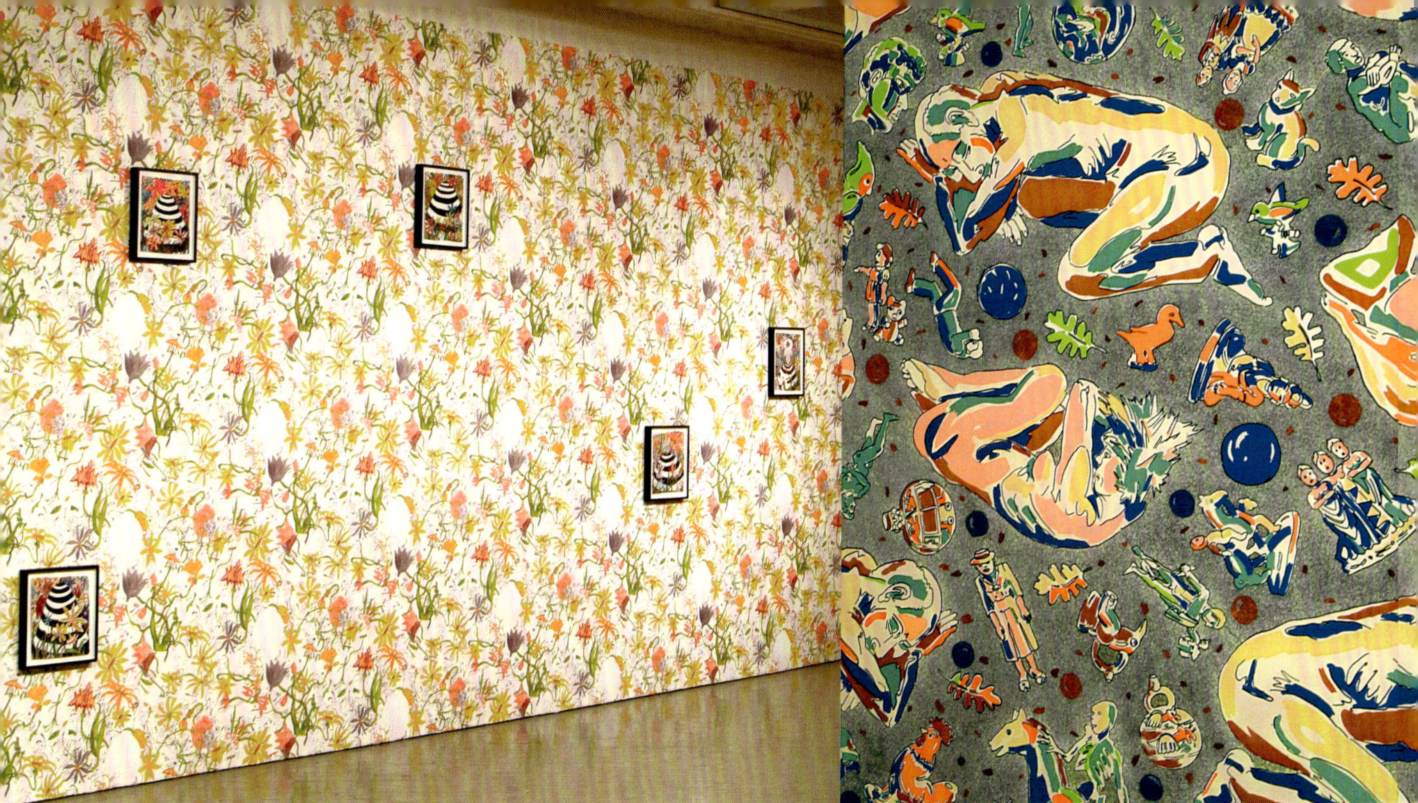

Jorge Pardo
American, b. Cuba, 1963
Untitled (room installation), 1999
Wallpaper: hand screenprint on paper-backed cotton sateen, roll: 54 w.
Fabric: hand screenprint on linen and Swiss cotton, 55 1/4 to 56 w.
Upholstered furniture, pressboard video cabinet, lamps, pressboard and glass doors, cork floor, and birch plywood ceiling
Created in collaboration with The Fabric Workshop and Museum. Collection of The Fabric Workshop and Museum

Matthew Ritchie
British, b. 1964
The Warm Connection, 2003
Hand screenprint on wool felt, 36 x 24 1/2
Created in collaboration with The Fabric Workshop and Museum. Courtesy of the artist and The Fabric Workshop and Museum

Francesco Simeti
Italian and American, b. 1968
Arabian Nights and *Are You Ready?* wallpapers, 2003
Digital print on paper, roll: 19 5/8 w.; overall: 10′ x 16′8″
Created in collaboration with The RISD Museum. Courtesy of the artist and Galleria Massimo Minini, Brescia, and The RISD Museum

Kiki Smith
American, b. 1954
Weeping Willows Wallpaper, 2002–03
Hand screenprint on paper-backed cotton sateen, 45 x 55
Created in collaboration with The Fabric Workshop and Museum. Courtesy of the artist and The Fabric Workshop and Museum

Will Stokes
American, b. 1955
Leaves and Animals (wallpaper), 2003
Hand screenprint on paper-backed cotton sateen, roll 52 w.; partial roll: 25 x 52
Created in collaboration with The Fabric Workshop and Museum. Collection of The Fabric Workshop and Museum. Courtesy of the artist

Do-Ho Suh
Korean, b. 1962
Who Am We? (multi), 2000
Color offset print on paper, sheet: 24 x 36; overall: 10′ x 12′7″
Courtesy of the artist and Lehmann Maupin Gallery, New York

Rosemarie Trockel
German, b. 1952
Eiweiss, 1998
Flocking (glue, wool particles) on paper; roll: 27 w.; overall: 82 x 27
Courtesy of *nest* products

Andy Warhol
American, 1928–87
Cow Wallpaper (two colorways), 1966; refabricated for the Andy Warhol Museum, Pittsburgh, 1994
Hand screenprint on paper, roll: 180 x 28
Blue/yellow colorway, overall: 11′1″ x 30′10″
Pink/yellow colorway, overall: 10′ x 20′
Courtesy of the Andy Warhol Museum, Pittsburgh

Mao Wallpaper, 1974; refabricated for the Andy Warhol Museum, Pittsburgh, 1994
Hand screenprint on paper, roll: 180 x 28; overall: 10′ x 45′4″
Courtesy of the Andy Warhol Museum, Pittsburgh

Mao Tse-Tung (3 prints), 1972
Hand screenprint on paper, sheet: 36 x 36; framed: 41 1/2 x 40 1/2 (edition of 250)
Collection of Marion Boulton Stroud

Carrie Mae Weems
American, b. 1953
The Apple of Adam's Eye (folding screen), 1993
Pigment and silk embroidery on cotton sateen, Australian lacewood, 73 x 81 x 1 3/4 (edition 1/5)
Created in collaboration with The Fabric Workshop and Museum

Looking High and Low (wallpaper), from the "Africa Series," 1993
Hand screenprint on paper, roll: 180 x 26 1/2; overall: 10′ x 17′4″ and 10′ x 11′
Collection of The Fabric Workshop and Museum

William Wegman
American, b. 1943
Alphabet Border (wallpaper), 1993
Hand screenprint on paper, roll: 13 1/2 x 360; overall: 8′1″ x 13′8″
Courtesy of the artist and A/D Gallery, New York

Rob Wynne
American, b. 1950
Eyes Wallpaper, 2003
Hand screenprint on paper, roll: 50 w.; overall: 10′ x 35′
Courtesy of the artist

Flies, 1999-2001
Lustre-glazed ceramic, 16 x 12 x 4 each
Courtesy of the artist

English
Wallpaper fragment, 19th century
25 1/2 x 21 1/16
Gift of Miss Grace Lincoln Temple, 1921-58-4

William Morris, designer
English, 1834-96
For Morris and Company
London, England, 1861-1940
Arthur Sanderson and Sons, Ltd., manufacturers
London, England, est. 1860
"Poppy" Wallpaper, first printed 1881;
20th-century reprint
22 x 22
Gift of Mrs. Anthony Garvan, 1970-129-6b

Attrib. to C.F.A. Voysey
English, 1857-1941
Charles Knowles and Company, manufacturers
England
Wallpaper fragment, printed ca. 1903
37 x 22
Gift of Mrs. Anthony Garvan, 1970-129-13

Made by M. H. Birge and Sons
Buffalo, New York, est. 1878
Wallpaper fragment, early 20th century
26 x 22
Gift of the Horace N. Pryor Company,
1970-170-36b

M. H. Birge and Sons, manufacturers
Buffalo, New York, est. 1878
Wallpaper fragment
26 x 22
Gift of the Horace N. Pryor Company,
1970-170-87

M. H. Birge and Sons, manufacturers
Buffalo, New York, est. 1878
Wallpaper fragment, early 20th century
24 1/2 x 21 1/2
Gift of the Horace N. Pryor Company,
1970-170-7d

American
Wallpaper fragment, early 20th century
20 11/16 x 26
Gift of William Sumner Appleton, 1920-88-2

American
Wallpaper fragment, early 20th century
22 x 22
Gift of the Horace N. Pryor Company,
1970-170-64

Thomas Strahan Co., manufacturers
Chelsea, Massachusetts
Wallpaper fragment, early 20th century
32 1/8 x 22
Gift of the Horace N. Pryor Company,
1970-170-122

Thomas Strahan Co., manufacturers
Chelsea, Massachusetts
Wallpaper fragment
32 x 22
Gift of the Horace N. Pryor Company,
1970-170-116

BELOW: Glenn Ligon at FWM, *Untitled*, 2003, hand screenprint on acrylic and paper. Created in collaboration with The Fabric Workshop and Museum. Collection of The Fabric Workshop and Museum

FACING PAGE: Kiki Smith at FWM, *Weeping Willows Wallpaper*, 2003, hand screenprint on paper-backed cotton sateen. Created in collaboration with The Fabric Workshop and Museum. Courtesy of the artist and The Fabric Workshop and Museum. Image by Matthew Suib

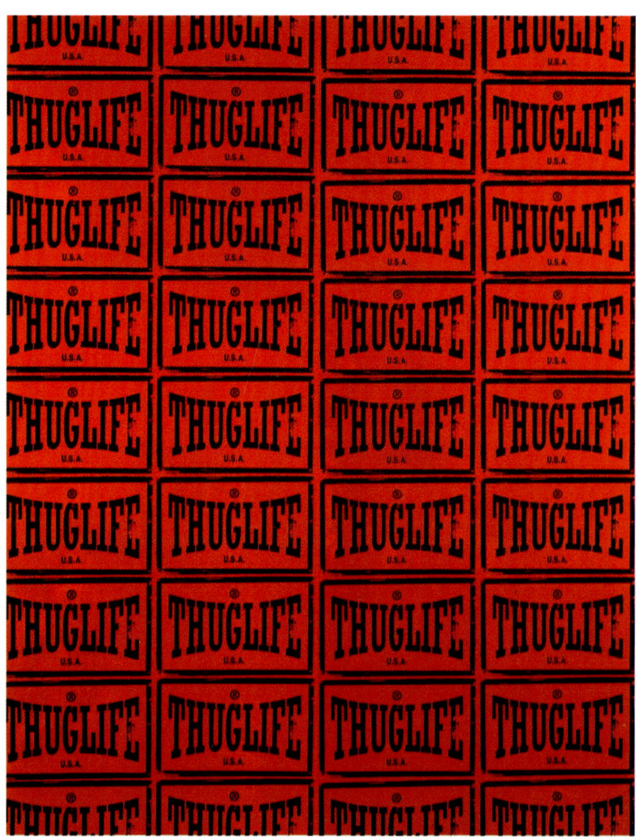

Photography Credits

Will Brown
Photographer
Pages 8, 15, 24 (bottom image), 53 (bottom image), 56

Erik Gould
Staff Photographer
The RISD Museum, Providence
Inside front cover and pages 2, 5, 6, 18, 21, 22 (bottom image), 26, 27, 28, 29, 30, 31, 33 (upper image), 38 (bottom image), 44, 50, 51

Aaron Igler
Manager of Visual Media and Technology
The Fabric Workshop and Museum, Philadelphia
Cover and pages 9, 10, 11, 12, 13, 14, 17, 23, 32, 34, 41, 43, 45, 46, 47, 49, 53 (top image), 54, 55, 56, 57, 58, 59, inside back cover

BELOW: Adam Cvijanovic at FWM, *Backyard* (detail), 2002, Flasche, acrylic, and latex on Tyvek (synthetic sheeting). Courtesy of the artist and Bellwether Gallery, Brooklyn

FACING PAGE: Nicole Eisenman at FWM, *Gray Bar Hotel*, 2003, hand screenprint on paper-backed cotton sateen. Created in collaboration with The Fabric Workshop and Museum. Collection of The Fabric Workshop and Museum

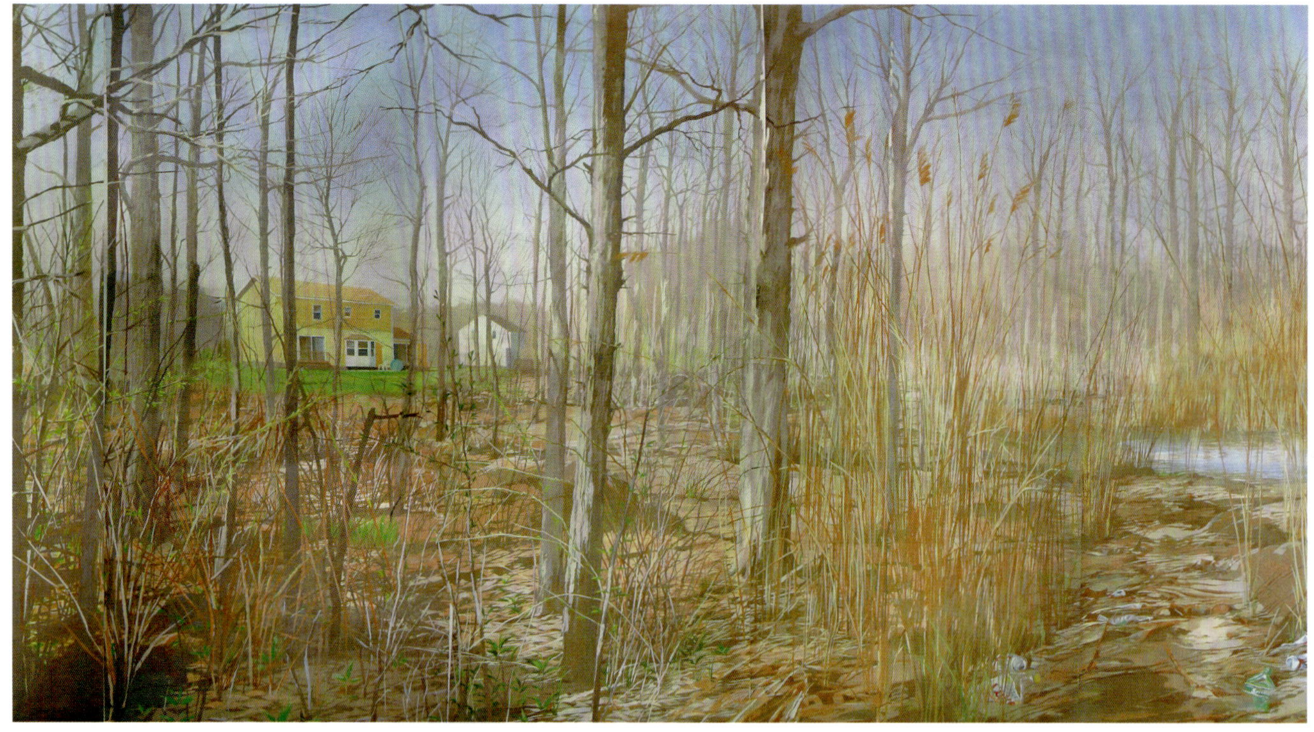